P9-DDD-152

FROGS

FROGS

A Wildlife Handbook

Kim Long

Johnson Books
BOULDER

Published in the United States by Johnson Books, a division of Johnson Publishing Company, 1880 South 57th Court, Boulder, Colorado 80301. EMAIL books@jpcolorado.com

9 8 7 6 5 4 3 2 1

Cover design: Margaret Donharl
Cover illustration: Kim Long

"A Fable by Aesop," page 2 ©1998 Gregory McNamee.
"Foreign Frog Calls," page 156 ©1996–1998 Catherine N. Ball.

All illustrations by the author unless otherwise indicated.

Library of Congress Cataloging-in-Publication Data
    Long, Kim.
        Frogs: a wildlife handbook / Kim Long
            p. cm. — (Johnson nature series)
        Includes bibliographical references and index.
        ISBN 1-55566-226-9 (pbk. : alk. paper)
        1. Frogs. I. Title. II. Series: Long, Kim. Johnson nature series
        QL668.E2L655 1999   98-55481
        597.8'9—dc21   CIP

Printed in the United States by
Johnson Printing
1880 South 57th Court
Boulder, Colorado 80301

CONTENTS

ACKNOWLEDGMENTS

Dr. Randall Lockwood, Humane Society of the U.S.

Christopher Richard, Oakland Museum of California

Dr. Joseph T. Collins,
     The Center for North American Amphibians and Reptiles

Gregory McNamee

Catherine N. Ball

Kathleen Cain

Pat Wagner and Leif Smith

The Bloomsbury Review

Denver Public Library

Norlin Library, University of Colorado

Auraria Library, Metropolitan State College

The Tattered Cover

"Spring again. Frogs in a deep gurgling chorus."
— John Muir (journal entry, April 13, 1870)

INTRODUCTION

Frogs are so obvious, yet they can be hard to see, hidden within their surroundings. These hopping amphibians are widespread throughout the world, appearing in a variety of urban settings and natural habitats. Like a natural clock, they are one of the first signs of spring, heard if not seen soon after ice and snow melt away.

Like many of nature's most fascinating creatures, however, those most obvious are sometimes the most overlooked. Unfortunately for frogs, they have recently begun to attract much attention, but not because of their unique sounds, shapes, colors, habits, or metamorphosis. Instead, these amphibians are the center of attention due to an increasing frequency of disfiguring defects, malformations that may signal something seriously wrong with the environment they inhabit, an environment that often suffers from the growing pains of the human population.

Despite this interference, these amphibians have thrived for millions of years, taking advantage of their habitat in a way unlike any other form of animal. In earlier eras, curious observers took advantage of frogs to study the mystery of life. From the first microscope to the development of modern anatomy, human knowledge has benefited from the wonders of this small lifeform. Whether their future is threatened or not, this may be the right time to examine frogs anew, learning more about what makes them unique and gaining new appreciation for the way nature works, from the structure of individual animals to the interaction of animals with their environments. In this book, the focus is on frogs, but this is not meant to slight the equally interesting subject of toads. Much of the contents, especially about metamorphosis and diet, applies equally to both.

Readers should note that the scientific naming conventions used in this book conform to the latest information published in 1997 by the Society for the Study of Amphibians and Reptiles. Some amphibian field guides may not follow this system, leading to possible confusion.

THE STORY OF FROGS

"I would on first setting out, inform the reader that there is a much greater number of miracles and natural secrets in the frog than anyone hath every before thought of or discovered." — Jan Swammerdam (1637–1680)

Frogs appear in legend and folklore in many cultures throughout history. Although some of these ancient and modern symbols are meant to be negative, most of the time frogs are portrayed as friendly and even helpful to humans. Toads, however, often end up in the opposite category, represented as dirty, malicious, and even evil.

In ancient China, the Spirit of the Green Frog was one of many minor deities. According to Chinese mythology, this creature was fond of wine, feasting, and theatricals. Carved figures of the frog spirit were used for special purposes, including curing deafness. Those seeking this cure would make an offering of wine to the frog spirit. The frog spirit was popular in many parts of China, particularly those along the Yangtze valley and wherever lakes and rivers offered suitable habitat for these amphibians.

The frog is a potent symbol in traditional Chinese culture. The Chinese called the frog the "heavenly chicken," because frog spawn were thought to fall from heaven along with the dew. Frogs also represent wealth and were depicted on good-luck charms.

A Chinese legend about frogs is associated with Liu Hsi (4 B.C.–57 A.D.), the Minister of State during the reign of the King of Yen. Fired for being too frank, Liu Hsi wandered the country searching for the Pill of Immortality. Hundreds of years later, he reappeared as a servant to a wealthy family. One day, he pulled a frog from the well, a frog he claimed to have been seeking for a long time. While a crowd watched, he and the frog floated into the air and disappeared.

In some Chinese regions, special temples were built just for frogs. Frog temples were traditionally used for worship by local officials when they were first placed in office. In these temples, live frogs were encouraged to stay with offerings of food and water. On occasion, these pampered animals would wander away from their appointed homes. When found, they would be brought back to the temple accompanied by drums and music.

A Sanskrit story from ancient India depicts Bhekî, the frog, as a beautiful young woman. One day, while she was sitting next to a well, a king discovered her and asked her to marry him. Bhekî agreed, but only if the king agreed to one condition, never to show her any water, not even a single drop. One day at a later time, she felt tired and asked the king to bring her some water and forgetting his promise, he complied. Bhekî then disappeared. This story is an allegory referring to the Sun, which when it was low in the sky and touched the horizon, appeared to squat like a frog.

Many cultures have myths and folktales that involve a frog as an ugly animal that is transformed into a handsome man, usually through the intervention of a beautiful woman. "The Frog Princess," one of the best known of the Grimm fairy tales, is an example of this kind. Similar stories are found from India, Hungary, Norway, Germany, England, and Native American tribes.

2

More modern, but equally well known, is a popular tale about a frog wooing a mouse. Dating from at least the early 1600s in England, the earliest version of this story was published as "A Moste Strange Weddinge of the Frogge and the Mouse," and much later as "The Frog Went a-Courting."

In ancient Egypt, carvings and religious statues were made in the image of frogs. Archeologists have also discovered embalmed frogs in some Egyptian burial sites. To Ptah, the creator of the universe and everything in it, the frog was sacred. Other Egyptian gods were depicted with the head of a frog, including Keh, and Nau. Heket, the goddess of birth, also had a frog as her companion animal. The Romans associated frogs with Venus because of their abundant fertility.

Among Australian aborigines, a mythical being represented by a frog was known as a great dancer, better even than the crow. The frog also sang songs in a wonderful bass voice and was a clever ventriloquist.

Ancient Greece fostered a rich tradition of animal fantasies.

FROG FESTIVAL

In Japan, the Kaeru Tobi, or Frog Festival, is held every year on July 7 at the Zaodo Temple in Nara. This ceremony honors a traditional Japanese legend, the story of a young man who said bad things about a yamabushi, a Buddhist priest, and was turned into a frog. During the festival, statues of a frog are carried around the local community.

One of the most famous to have survived is *The Batrachomyomachy*, "The War Between the Frogs and the Mice." A satire, the work pokes fun at the *Iliad*, a much earlier and more famous piece of Greek literature. In the *Batrachomyomachy*, frog people go to war with the mice people because of the abduction of Pricharpax, the mouse heroine, by Physignathos, the frog king. After some ups and downs for both sides, the god Zeus intervenes on behalf of the frogs by sending them crabs as allies. The entire saga spanned one day.

Another important piece of Greek literature about frogs was *Batrachoi,* "The Frogs," a comedic play written by Aristophanes. *The Frogs* used animals to make fun of humans and in particular, Euripides, a Greek poet whom Aristophanes didn't like. In his play, the author is credited with the first use in literature of phonetic imitations of real animal sounds. Here, a group of frogs performs a chorus, singing "Brekekekex, koax, koax." (For a list of how foreign languages depict the sound of frogs, see "Foreign Frog Calls," page 156.)

Chest ornament depicting a female frog worn by a medicine man in the Arawak Indian tribe from northeastern South America.

Illustration from the *30th Annual Report* of the Bureau of American Ethnology, published in 1915.

In South and Central America, where frogs were a common part of the environment, they were often associated with rain. Members of some tribes kept a few frogs in their dwellings, where they were used to predict when rain would come. In Japan and Vietnam, frogs were also linked to rain or the rainy season.

Among the Carib tribes, the croaking of the rain frog, "kobono-aru," meant the coming of rain. Most importantly, the frog was the god of the waters, and to some tribes was too revered to kill or eat, but frogs might be held captive to help bring on the rain. In some cases, the frogs were beaten or whipped in order to make it rain. The Caribs also believed that the first frog had special powers; fire came from her mouth, cassava from her neck and shoulders, and she introduced music to the people and showed them how to hunt.

The Lenca, a culture native to Honduras, describe how the deer got its shape in a creation myth. According to this legend, the deer had completed forming its body but was not satisfied with how it looked. To become complete, it stole two bumps from the head of a frog, which were transformed into the deer's antlers. But because

4

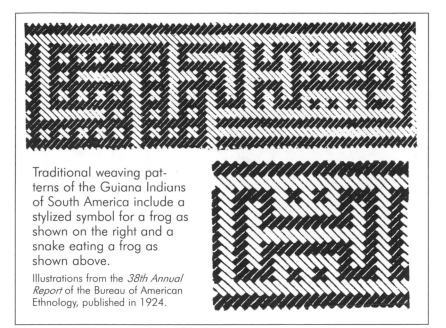

Traditional weaving patterns of the Guiana Indians of South America include a stylized symbol for a frog as shown on the right and a snake eating a frog as shown above.

Illustrations from the *38th Annual Report* of the Bureau of American Ethnology, published in 1924.

the antlers were stolen, they keep falling off and the deer has to repeat the process every year.

In Nepal, a demon known as Ghanta Karna roams the land and creates havok. Ghanta Karna wears bells in his ears — his name means "Bell Ears" — in order to drown out the name of Lord Vishnu, which, if heard, would reform his evil ways. But one force that can vanquish this demon is a god in the form of a frog. In a traditional Nepalese story, the frog tricks Ghanta Karna into jumping into a well, thereby allowing people to hit him with sticks.

In most cultures, frogs have been thought of as a positive force, representing something for the common good. A number of ancient cultures — including those in Egypt, Greece, Italy, and Turkey, among others — went even further, using the image of the frog on amulets and charms for good luck. In Burma, children are traditionally protected against the "evil eye" by wearing amulets in the shape of a frog.

In Ghana, the Ewe culture holds an annual Yam Festival that

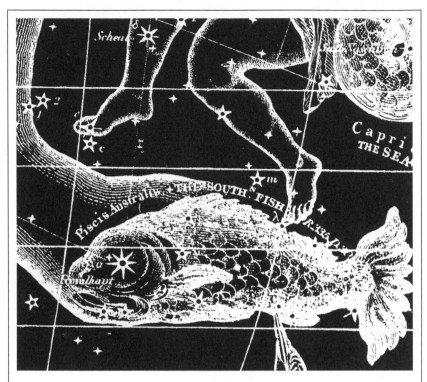

THE FROG STARS

Arabic astronomers named two stars after frogs. One was called Al Difdi' al Awwal, the First Frog. This name was later changed to Fum al Ḥūt, the Fish's Mouth. It marks the eye of the constellation Piscis Austrinus, the Southern Fish, and is the brightest star in this group. In the modern system of star names, it is Alpha Piscis Austrini, and the common name has been condensed to Fomalhaut. Fomalhaut was an important star to astronomical observers because of its brightness; it is one of the twenty brightest stars in the sky. The other star is Al Difdi' al Thāni, the Second Frog. Today, it is known in the west as Rana Secunda. This illustration is from a star atlas published by Elijah Hindsdale Burritt in 1833.

includes an important purification ritual. The local priest creates a magic bundle by tying a chicken and a frog to a sprig from a palm oil tree. This bundle, called the atidzie, is used to "sweep" the town, then laid on a heap of ashes in the main street. There, its magic keeps evil from entering the town.

One of the symbols of France and a former symbol of many French kings is the fleur-de-lis, a stylized image of the iris. Originally, however, this design was depicted as a group of three frogs, a common animal in the muddy streets of early Paris.

In old England, the frog was often seen as a "spirit of the well," guarding this source of water. In a few creation myths, the world is supported on the back of a frog. In other places, the frog also symbolized inquisitiveness because of its bulging eyes, inspiration, renewed birth, and fertility. Also, it could represent abundance and eternal life, the latter because before the life cycle of the frog was understood, it was thought to appear and disappear endlessly. It could, however, also be a negative symbol. In some cultures and situations, the frog symbolized pestilence, vain opinions, and in dreams, indiscretion. In Japan, the symbol is of perseverance and energy. In Tatar mythology, it was a frog that discovered the sacred mountain. From there, he brought back birch and stones to the people, from which the first fire was produced.

NATIVE AMERICAN FROGS

"On the summit of white Nḡiwolik
There the green frogs are singing.
Lying near the blue storm clouds
There many frogs are singing." — Pima song

Native Americans, like other cultures throughout the world, generally held the frog in high esteem. For most, it was a symbol of rain and water, natural forces that often defined the difference between life and death. Particularly for tribes with well-developed agricultural systems — from the Choctaw of the southeast to the Hopi of the southwest — this symbol was a critical aspect of seasonal change and the success or failure of crops. The Iroquois, on the other hand, were one of a few tribes that thought of the frog as a symbol of aridness.

Like other animals that were common in regional environments, frogs figured prominently in Indian mythology. A Nez Perce myth tells of a frog widow who was mistreated by her people. In anger, she went to the source of the people's river and sat in it, stopping the flow of water. Although the people did not connect the disappearance of the frog widow with the drying of the river's flow, Coyote figured out what must have happened. He journeyed up the river bed, making five rafts along the way. When he found the frog widow, he pulled her up, allowing the water to flow once again, and then tossed her into the running stream, exclaiming "This is the way you will always be: whenever high water comes, it will always carry frogs down the river." Coyote, meanwhile, was saved from the water by one of his rafts.

Another Nez Perce myth pits Coyote against Frog. Frog had devised a unique race in which he ran up one side of a smooth pole while any bird that challenged him raced up the other. The first animal to reach the top got to cut off the other's head. Because Frog

8

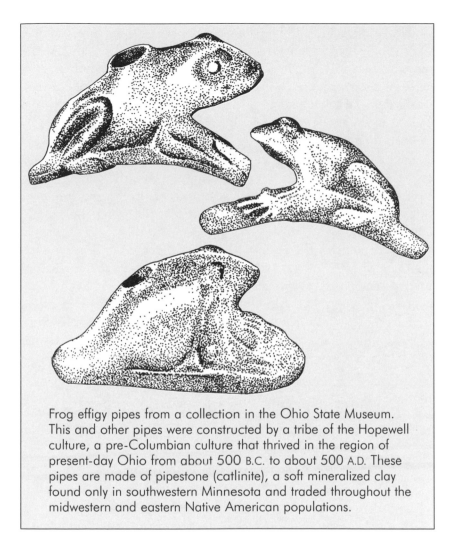

Frog effigy pipes from a collection in the Ohio State Museum. This and other pipes were constructed by a tribe of the Hopewell culture, a pre-Columbian culture that thrived in the region of present-day Ohio from about 500 B.C. to about 500 A.D. These pipes are made of pipestone (catlinite), a soft mineralized clay found only in southwestern Minnesota and traded throughout the midwestern and eastern Native American populations.

had figured out which side of the pole was the fastest, he always won and got to kill all the birds that raced against him. Then Coyote got involved, convincing Bluejay to enter the race. Bluejay was the first to the top because he flew part of the way, and as the winner, killed Frog.

A Nez Perce story describes why there is a Frog in the Moon.

Originally, Frog and another woman were wives to the Sun. Sun was so hot that the people held a meeting to decide what to do. At the meeting, Sun told Frog to sit on his eye, which she did, dimming the sunlight. Alarmed, the people tried to pull Frog off of Sun, but they could not make her budge. So Coyote changed the Sun into the Moon, and now the Moon has the image of Frog on his face.

According to Cherokee myth, a great frog in the sky would occasionally swallow the Sun and the Moon, causing an eclipse. Whenever the sky began to grow dark during the day, the people would rush to create loud noises. They would beat drums and fire their rifles in order to scare away this great frog, allowing the Sun to emerge again.

Among many of the pueblo cultures — located in a geographic region with little annual rainfall — frogs and tadpoles were often used as symbols that were linked to the power of water. In the Zuni pueblo, the traditional rain chief used a frog fetish as a rain caller. In both the Zuni and Hopi pueblos, fetishes are religious talismans, small carvings that are said to be real animals transfigured to stone or clay. In the Taos pueblo, one of the major mythological figures is

SONG OF THE OKOGIES IN SPRING

See how the white spirit presses us,
Presses us, presses us, heavy and long, —
Presses us down to the frost-bitten earth.
Alas! you are heavy, ye spirits so white,
Alas! you are cold, you are cold, you are cold.
Ah! cease, shining spirits that fell from the skies,
Ah! cease so to crush us, and keep us in dread;
Ah! when will you vanish and Seegwun return.

This song about frogs (okogies) is attributed to Ba-bahm-wa-na-geghig-equa, possibly a member of an Allegheny tribe. It was published in 1884 in the book *Indian Myths*, by Ellen R. Emerson. In the last line, Seegwun is a word for Spring.

SIGN LANGUAGE

Among some North American tribes, the word for frog could be "spoken" with the hands in a universal sign language understood across many cultures. To make the sign for frog:

"Hold partially-compressed right hand, back down, in front of, close to, and little above mouth, fingers pointing to left and upwards; move the hand downwards, turning palm towards mouth [this sequence is also the sign for the word "water"]... then compress the right hand, hold it back to right, in front of and little lower than shoulder; move it to front on a curve upwards to front and downwards, imitating motion of frog jumping."

From *The Indian Sign Language*, by W.P. Clark, published in 1885 by L.R. Hamersly & Company.

Big Water Man, a huge figure in the shape of a frog. Big Water Man wields a punishing power, a force that can bring floods or landslides.

Although frogs had this special association with water, an important one because of its life-giving power, many Native Americans included them as a regular part of their diet. Even if held in high regard as symbols, they might still be part of a local menu. But some tribes were known to avoid eating frogs, adding them to lists of taboo foods. And some tribes avoided killing them, as this was thought to bring bad luck and could have a negative influence on hoped-for rain. Among the Thompson River Indians, however, the reverse held true. This tribe sought to influence rain by killing frogs.

Among the Hidatsa, the frog was considered one of seven water spirits, along with the otter, the beaver, the turtle, the mink, the muskrat, and some kinds of snakes. The snakes were associated with major rivers, guarding them and protecting the water level, but frogs were linked to some streams, ponds, and springs. In order to determine which water spirit lived in a specific water source, a member of the tribe followed a fasting ritual to reveal its image. The Mewan Indians of central California also considered frogs part of their spiritual lineup. To this tribe, the wife of Coyote man was Ko-tó-lah, Frog Woman.

Creek tribes also associated frogs with the power of water. Sacred bundles were spiritually tied to the spirits living in tributaries of the Missouri River. These bundles contained beaver fur and claws, the skins of muskrat, mink, and otter, turtle shells, buffalo skulls, roots, and various types of native plants, along with dried frogs. To the Creeks, the frog spirit was responsible for teaching them a special song used for doctoring. The Kwakiutl tribe, located in the wet regions of the northwest, used the frog to symbolize physical force; they had a special war dance associated with the frog and a frog whistle.

In the Navajo creation myth, First Man and First Woman lived in a hogan in the first world, the lowest underworld. To their east lived Tiéholtsodi, the water monster; to their west lived Ácihi Están, Salt Woman; to the north was Cqaltláqale, the Blue Heron; and to the south was Tcal', the Frog, who lived in a house of blue fog.

From the culture of the Kutenai comes the myth of Antelope and Frog. Antelope was the chief of a town and the fastest runner, able to beat anyone in a foot race. In another town, Frog was chief and he devised a plan to beat Antelope. Frog challenged Antelope to a race, with the winner awarded the other's property. Before the race, Frog gathered all his family and all the frogs that lived in his town and went to the trail where the race was to be held. There, he had each frog place itself in front of another, each one jump apart. When the race started, Frog made one jump, leaping ahead to where the next frog sat on the trail. That frog then leaped one jump, and so on, all the way to the turnaround point and back again. As fast as Antelope ran, it seemed that Frog was always one leap ahead of him, and he ran harder and harder trying to keep up. When he reached the finish line, out of breath, it was just behind Frog.

A Tlingit myth tells of a large town near a big lake that was full of frogs. In the town, the chief's daughter spoke badly to the frogs, making fun of them. One night, she was approached by a young man who asked her to marry him. Even though she had already rejected many marriage proposals, she quickly accepted his offer and went with him to his father's house, which appeared in the center of the lake. To the people of the town, she seemed to disappear and after no one could find where she went, they began a period of mourning. The next spring, a man from the town saw the missing woman sitting with the frogs in the middle of the lake. The people from the town brought food and other offerings to the frogs, hoping to persuade them to let the woman come back to them, but the frogs refused to let her go. Then the people dug ditches around the lake, draining the water. As the water rushed away, it carried off the frogs and the woman, who was quickly grabbed. But even though

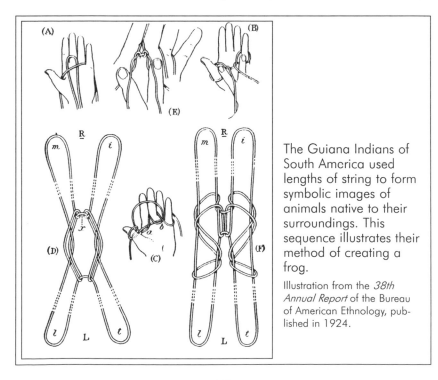

The Guiana Indians of South America used lengths of string to form symbolic images of animals native to their surroundings. This sequence illustrates their method of creating a frog.

Illustration from the *38th Annual Report* of the Bureau of American Ethnology, published in 1924.

13

she was back home with her people, she did not eat and soon died. Because the frogs at this place had lived with the woman, the people said that they understood the language of people.

One Cherokee myth describes how all the animals of the earth became disgusted with people. Not only were there getting to be too many of them, but they had invented spears, arrows, and other weapons that made it easier to kill the animals. The animals got together in various groups to figure out how to respond. The birds, insects, and small animals met in one of these councils, with the grubworm as chief. Each animal in turn got to give its opinion of the problem and vote on whether Man was guilty of cruelty and injustice to them; seven votes would be enough to condemn. The first to speak was Frog. "We must do something to check the increase of the race, or people will become so numerous that we shall be crowded from off the earth. See how they have kicked me about because I'm ugly, as they say, until my back is covered with sores." After all the animals spoke, the vote was almost unanimous, "Guilty!" They decided the right punishment was to devise diseases that would kill people. But the plants, who were friends of the people, heard about this plan and each tree, shrub, herb, grass, and moss agreed to offer a cure for one of the diseases the animals had created.

FROG SUPERSTITIONS

"The frog in the well is best left where he is."

— traditional Chinese proverb

One of the most familiar animals throughout the natural world, frogs have also long been associated with supernatural forces and strange powers. Because they are so closely linked to water and are usually linked to warm seasons, popular beliefs about frogs often reflected a desire to have greater control over Mother Nature.

Beliefs about rain, for example, are one of the major superstitions that involve frogs. Throughout the world, folk tales and superstitions relate how the sound or sight of frogs indicates coming rain. In some cases, it is the number of frog calls that determines the chance of rain. Frogs gathering close to a house might also be a sign of rain. Variations of this concept are also used to foretell the arrival of spring. Before spring really arrives, for instance, a frog must be heard croaking three times.

In India, girls would kill frogs to bring luck and enhance their chance of marriage. In early European cultures, a jumping frog was a sign of bad luck to couples newly married. The Arawaks believed that a certain kind of spotted frog had special powers. Pregnant women would tickle this kind of frog to make it jump and depending on how it landed, it would tell her whether her child would be a boy or a girl.

Frogs have also long been used as a means of controlling or curing the physical ailments of humans. Soup made from nine frogs was thought to cure whooping cough, or in another superstition, this ailment could be treated by hanging a frog's leg around the neck of the afflicted person. If a soup were made from three different kinds of frogs, it would prevent epileptic seizures. Frog soup was also recommended as a cure for croup in children. To treat thrush, the head of a young frog was to be held in the mouth of the patient.

As a cure for gout, a frog was caught when neither the Moon or

15

the Sun were in the sky. The back legs of the frog were cut off and wrapped in deerskin. The severed right limb was placed on the afflicted person's right foot; the severed left limb was placed on the left foot.

According to folk wisdom in many parts of the world, frogs and toads are a common cause of warts. Some people believe that just touching a frog will cause warts, but there are also many variations on this theme. For instance, if you keep a frog more than six days, you will get warts; if a frog urinates on you, it will cause warts; frog saliva will generate warts; step on a frog, you'll get warts; spit at a frog, expect warts to appear. But frogs could also provide a remedy for this affliction. One folk cure was to impale a frog on a stick and rub its skin over the warts. When the frog died, the warts were gone.

Frogs also could produce other problems of the skin. In parts of Europe, boils on the left hand were thought to come from touching green frogs and boils on the right hand came from brown frogs.

For eye diseases, one folk cure was to tie a live frog to the forehead. To remove freckles, a live frog was rubbed over them. Children could be cured of bedwetting by tying a frog to the child's leg at night. To stop a rash from spreading, a frog was cut in half and tied to the rash. Snakebite venom could be drawn out by placing a frog on the puncture. Burned to ashes, frogs could also be used to remove unwanted hair. One widespread belief that persisted into the twentieth century was that cancer could be cured if the cancer sufferer swallowed young frogs.

Farm animals were also thought to benefit from frog therapy. For a sheep afflicted with "wind" — the production of excess gas in the digestive system — a touted cure was to tie a live frog to the sheep. When the frog died, the wind was gone.

Even in modern times, frogs have been connected to superstition. In parts of Scotland and England early in the twentieth century, for example, a "magic" frog bone was used to help keep unruly farm horses under control. Such a magic bone was produced by catching a frog, killing it, and smashing the body. The gory remains were

FROG LUCK

Many frog superstitions that have been part of North American cultures came from various cultures in Europe, Asia, and Africa, arriving along with immigrants and slaves. Such superstitions have been part of folklore in New England, the South, and the Midwest for a hundred years or more.

- If you see a frog on the road, it means good luck.
- If a frog comes into your home, it means good luck.
- If you make a wish after seeing the first frog in the spring, the wish will come true.
- Because frogs are possessed with the souls of dead children, killing a frog brings bad luck.
- If a frog sees your teeth, you'll have bad luck.
- If a frog is killed, a farmer's cow will produce bloody milk.
- If you kill a frog, a cow will die.
- If you kill a frog, you will stub your toe.
- If a pregnant woman looks into a well while drawing water, her child will be born with a frog face.
- If a pregnant woman dreams about a frog, her child will be born with only one toe on each foot and only one finger on each hand.
- If a woman spits into a frog's mouth, she won't get pregnant.

thrown into a flowing stream and any bones that floated upstream were collected, dried, and infused with aromatic herbs. Supposedly, the empowered bone possessed a special force.

In the Caribbean and parts of North America, hoodoo practices also utilize frogs for special power in magic rituals. This type of folk religion includes the use of mojos, also known as conjure bags, that can contain roots, herbs, animal parts, dyed feathers, coins, and other items. Dried frogs are included in mojos intended to promote fertility and sexual potency.

Some superstitions and religious beliefs about frogs are intended to promote avoidance. Among the Karma people of New Guinea, frogs are a major part of the diet, but not all of the time. When boys are in a critical age period — between the time when their noses are pierced and the end of their tribal initiation rites — they are forbidden to eat frogs or tadpoles. In the same culture, younger children are not allowed to eat some kinds of tree frogs because it is thought the frogs will stop the growing process.

The Cherokee Indians of North America believed that the common green frog caused warts to appear on people. The Cherokee word for wart is the same as for green frog, "walâ'si." Traditionally, Cherokees ate frogs but had one taboo regarding this kind of meat. Tribal ball players who were in training were not supposed to eat them because it was thought that the brittleness of the frog bones would be passed on, weakening the athletes.

FROG NAMES

"In these frogs, then, we have beautiful, harmless, useful, and cheerful, if not, strictly speaking, musical animals. Is not their title to our good wishes well established?"

— Charles C. Abbott
(1884, *A Naturalist's Rambles About Home*)

Frogs, like all animals, have more than one set of names. To biologists, they are first and most accurately given a scientific name, a tag created to fit into a conventional, worldwide system that helps keep individual species separate from one another. But frogs also have a history of common names, some rising from popular usage and others as earlier forms of scientific description. Unlike the scientific method, common names may sometimes overlap, with the same frog called different names by different people or different frogs named alike in different regions.

Names are often derived by the person who first observed or collected the animal, sometimes with the person's name either in its original form or "Latinized." Names may also be derived from geographical locations, the place where the animal was first discovered or the region where it is most commonly found. Other naming conventions include habitats — swamp, mountain, pond, etc. — and physical characteristics — including colors, vocal calls, or activity.

FROG IS THE WORD

The modern word "frog" in English was derived from an earlier form, "frogge." This was the word in Middle English — a previous form of English that was used from about 1000 A.D. to the 1400s — and before that, it was "frogga" in Old English — the form used from about 600 A.D. to about 1000 A.D. Before English developed, the word had a previous existence, as "frauki" or "froskr" in Old Norse and "frosk" in Old High German.

THE LANGUAGE OF FROGS

AFRIKAANS padda
ALBANIAN zhabë
AMHARIC anqurarit
ARABIC ḍufdaεa
AYAPATHU thata
AZERBAIJANI qurbaga
BAMBARA ntori
BASQUE igel
BEMBA cûla
BENGALI byang
BYELORUSSIAN zhába
CATALAN granota
CHECHEN ph´id
CHINESE wa, chingwa
CHUMASH wakatsom
CROATIAN zaba
CZECHOSLOVAKIAN zába
DANISH frø
DUTCH kikvors, kikker
ESPERANTO frogo
FINNISH sammakko
FRENCH grenouille
GAELIC losgann
GERMAN frosch
GREEK batrachos
GUARANI ju'i
HAUSA kwado
HAITIAN CREOLE krapo
HAWAIIAN poloka

HEBREW tsfarde
HINDI mēndhak
HMONG hma
HUNGARIAN béka
INDONESIAN kodok
INGUSH phwed
ITALIAN alamaro, rana
JAPANESE kaeru
KAZAKH qurbaqa
KIKUYU kiũra
KOREAN kaeguri
KHMER kong kype
KYRGYZ baka
LATIN rana
LATVIAN varde
LINGALA mombemba
LITHUANIAN varlė
MALAY katak
NEPALI bhyáguto
NEW PALAUAN dechédech
NIUE lane
NORWEGIAN frosk
PALI bheka
PHILIPINO palaká
PIDGIN rokrok
POLISH żaba
PORTUGUESE rã
PULAAR faaburu
ROMANIAN broasca

RUSSIAN	lyagushka	**TATAR**	baka
SAMOAN	rane	**THAI**	(l)gohp!
SANSCRIT	plava	**TIBETAN**	bagpa
SERBO-CROATIAN	zaba	**TURKISH**	kurbaga
SESOTHO	senqanqane	**UIGHUR**	paqa
SLOVAK	zaba	**UZBEK**	qurbaqa
SOMALI	rah, rake	**VIETNAMESE**	nhái
SPANISH	rana	**WELSH**	broga
SWAHILI	chura, vyura	**XHOSA**	isele
SWEDISH	groda	**YIDDISH**	zhabe
TAINO	coki'	**YORUBA**	àkèré

AMERICAN SIGN LANGUAGE

The sign for frog is made with the right hand. With the fingers closed in a fist, the right hand is held under the chin, palm facing in. The right index finger and the middle finger are then flicked out under the chin, signifying the jumping character of the frog.

TRUE FROGS

Most of the frogs that people actually see in North America are roughly grouped together into a category known as true frogs, part of the genus *Rana*. *Rana* is also the Latin word for frog.

BULLFROG *Rana catesbeiana*. Discovered in 1802 by George Shaw from a specimen collected in Charleston, South Carolina. The scientific name is a Latinized word honoring Mark Catesby, a prominent American naturalist in the 1700s who wrote one of the first books on the natural history of the country. Common names: bully, jug-o'-rum, North American bullfrog, American bullfrog. Spanish: rana mugidora, or rana grande. French Canadian: ouaouaron.

CARPENTER FROG *Rana virgatipes*. In 1891, Edward Cope found this species in Atlantic County, New Jersey. The species name is a combination

AMERICAN INDIAN LANGUAGES

ABENAKI	cegwal	**MAYAN**	ajkech'
ANISHINAABE	omakakii(g)	**MICMAC**	coqolsuwi, coqols
ARAPAHOE	maw xah baa hk	**MUSKOKEE**	kúte̅
ATAKAPA	aʹkitoc, aʹnenui	**NATICK**	tinógkukquas
BILOXI	kto^n, peska, tému	**NAVAJO**	ch'aɬ
BLACKFOOT	matsékapisàu	**OFO**	tému (bullfrog)
CHEROKEE	walosi	**OJIBWAY**	omaukkakee
CHEYENNE	oon'haï,	**ONONDAGA**	squárak
CHINOOK	shwahkuk	**OSAGE**	ṭ sébiuk̇'a
CHOCTAW	shukaṭti	**PAPAGO**	babad
COMANCHE	pasaviyió	**POTAWATOMI**	mukcako
DELAWARE	tsquallac	**SHOSHONE**	ya qua zah
HOPI	paaqwa	**SIOUX**	h'nahSH'KAH
KILIWI	x?nqhaatq	**TAKELMA**	lap'ãm
LAKOTA SIOUX	was' 'in	**TLINGIT**	x̣ix̣tc!

of two Latin words, "virga" for striped and "pes" for foot. Common names: Cope's frog, sphagnum frog.

CASCADES FROG *Rana cascadae*. In 1939, James R. Slater found and identified this species in the Ranier National Park in Washington. The species name is a Latinized word referring to the Cascade mountains. Common names: Slater's frog, Slater's spotted frog.

CHIRICAHUA LEOPARD FROG *Rana chiricahuensis*. Named in 1979 by U.S. biologists Platz and Mecham as a separate species of leopard frog. The name honors part of its home range, the Chiricahua mountains in southeastern Arizona. Another common name is the Chincahuw leopard frog. Spanish: rana de Chiricahua.

COLUMBIA SPOTTED FROG *Rana luteiventris*. The scientific name is derived from the Latin words for golden-yellow and belly, referring to this frog's color underneath. It was identified by H. Thompson in 1913 and previously known as the Nevada spotted frog.

CRAWFISH FROG *Rana areolata*. Discovered in Benton County, Indiana, in 1878 by F.L. Rice and N.S. Davis. The species name is a Latin word meaning something having a small open area. Common names include: gopher frog, northern gopher frog, crayfish frog, Hoosier frog, ring frog, Texas gopher frog, southern crayfish frog, and southern gopher frog.

FLORIDA BOG FROG *Rana okaloosae*. First identified as a separate species in 1985 by Paul Moler. The species name is a Latinized version of Okaloosa County, Florida, part of this frog's natural range.

FLORIDA LEOPARD FROG *Rana sphenocephala*. The species name is a combination of Greek words meaning wedge-shaped head. It was found in the vicinity of St. John's River, Florida, in 1886 by Edward D. Cope. Common names include southern meadow frog and southern leopard frog.

FOOTHILL YELLOW-LEGGED FROG *Rana boylei*. In 1854, Spencer Baird, founder of the U.S. National Museum, spotted this animal in Eldorado County, California. It was named after Dr. C.C. Boyle, a museum curator. Common names: western frog, Pacific frog, stink frog, Sierra Nevada yellow-legged frog, California yellow-legged frog, thick-skinned frog, Boyle's frog. Spanish: rana de pata amarilla.

GOPHER FROG *Rana capito*. Identified in 1855 by LeConte. "Capito" is a Latin word for one with a large head.

GREEN FROG *Rana clamitans*. "Clamitans" is a Latin word meaning loud-calling. Constantine Rafinesque, an amateur naturalist (and eccentric, he also identified and named twelve species of lightning and thunder) discovered the first specimen in 1820 in the area of Lake Champlain, New York. Common names: pond frog, spring frog, bawling frog, common spring

---

FROG WORDS

The word frog has been applied to many things, from other animals to pottery, including ...

frogbit, frog boot, frog cheese, frog crab, frog duck, frogeye, frogface, frogfish, frogger, froghopper, frog kick, frog lily, frogman, frogmarch, frog missile, frogmouth, frog pad, frog plant, frog's bladder, frog shell, frogskin, frog spit, frogsticker, frogstool, frog orchard, and frogfish.

For more information about the scientific classification of frogs, see page 88.

CLASS, ORDER, AND FAMILY NAMES

AMPHIBIA This word comes from the Greek word "amphibion," defined as double life, part spent on land and part in the water. The class Amphibia includes two orders, Caudata (salamanders and newts) and Anura (frogs and toads).

ANURA All frogs and toads are classified as members of this order. The name comes from Greek, and means "without tail."

RANIDAE The family for typical or "true" frogs. The word is a form of "rana," which is the Latin word for frog.

HYLIDAE This family group includes all treefrogs, cricket frogs, chorus frogs, and tropical frogs. The word comes from the Greek word "hyla," which means woods or forest.

frog, yellow-throated green frog, belly bumper, bully frog. French Canadian: grenouille verte.

LOWLAND LEOPARD FROG *Rana yavapaiensis*. Named for the site where the specimen was located, Yavapai County, Arizona. It was described as a separate species in 1984 by Platz and Frost. Spanish: rana de Yavapai.

MASLIN'S WOOD FROG *Rana maslini*. Separated from other species for the first time in 1969 by Maslin and named after him.

MINK FROG *Rana septentrionalis*. The species name is a Latin word meaning of the north, referring to the natural range of this frog. Common names: northern frog, Hoosier frog, Rocky Mountain frog. French Canadian: grenouille du Nord.

FROG SPOTS

Geographical locations in the United States named for the frog or bullfrog include more than 400 locations. "Frog" names on natural features of the landscape include places such as ...

- 1 bar
- 3 basins
- 3 bays
- 3 canyons
- 2 capes
- 1 cliff
- 7 flats
- 77 creeks and streams
- 6 islands

- 75 lakes
- 17 springs
- 15 summits
- 1 range
- 8 swamps
- 41 valleys
- 3 parks
- 6 ridges

MOUNTAIN YELLOW-LEGGED FROG *Rana muscosa.* Charles L. Camp discovered the first specimen near Pasadena, California, in 1919. The species name was coined from the Latin word "muscosus," meaning mossy, as a description of the camouflage on the frog's back. Common names: Sierra Madre yellow-legged frog, southern yellow-legged frog.

NORTHERN LEOPARD FROG *Rana pipiens.* Named in 1782 by H. Schreber from a frog caught in White Plains, New York. "Pipiens" is a Latin word meaning peeping. This first specimen came from a doctor serving with the British army during the Revolutionary War; he shipped the preserved specimen to Schreber in England. Common names: spring frog, spotted frog, water frog, shad frog, meadow frog. French Canadian: grenouille léopard.

OREGON SPOTTED FROG *Rana pretiosa.* This frog was discovered near Puget Sound, Washington, in 1853 by S.F. Baird and C. Girard. The species name is from the Latin word "pretiosus," meaning of great value.

Common names: Nevada spotted frog, western frog, Pacific frog, western spotted frog. French Canadian: grenouille maculée.

PICKEREL FROG *Rana palustris*. Named by John LeConte in 1825 from a specimen he discovered near Philadelphia, Pennsylvania. The name comes from the Latin word "paluster," meaning of the marsh. Common names include marsh frog, tiger frog, cold swamp frog, swamp frog, spring frog, and Le Conte's leopard frog. French Canadian: grenouille des marais.

PIG FROG *Rana grylio*. L. Stejneger identified this as a separate species in 1901. The species name is a version of the Latin word for cricket or grasshopper. Common names include: bullfrog, southern bullfrog, Joe Brown frog, swamp bullfrog, Bonnet's frog, lake frog, green bullfrog, and Florida bullfrog.

PLAINS LEOPARD FROG *Rana blairi*. This species is a recent discovery, taxonomically separated from other leopard frogs in 1973 by Mecham, Littlejohn, Oldham, Brown, and Brown. It was named in honor of Dr. W. Frank Blair, a distinguished zoology professor at the University of Texas.

RAMSEY CANYON LEOPARD FROG *Rana subaquavocalis*. One of the newest species of frogs to be recognized, this frog was created as a separate species in 1993 by American herpetologist Platz. The species name is a Latin combination that means underwater voice, referring to this frog's characteristic vocalization method.

RED-LEGGED FROG *Rana aurora*. In 1852, S.F. Baird and C. Girard found this frog near Puget Sound, Washington. The Latin word "aurora" means dawn and refers to the rosy color of this frog's legs. Common names: California red-legged frog, Drayton's frog, bullfrog, long-footed frog, Rocky Mountain frog, western wood frog, French frog, Leconte's frog, Oregon red-legged frog. Spanish: rana de patas roja. French-Canadian: grenouille à pattes rouges.

RELICT LEOPARD FROG *Rana onca*. Named in 1875 by Edward Cope, a paleontologist and an editor of the scientific publication *American Naturalist*. The species is named from the Greek word "onkos," meaning protuberance.

RIO GRANDE LEOPARD FROG *Rana berlandieri*. Described by Baird for the first time in 1859 and named for the location, near the Rio Grande River in southern Texas. The scientific name was coined to honor Jean Luis Berlandieri, a Belgian naturalist who spent years living and researching in Mexico in the nineteenth century. Spanish: rana leopardo.

RIVER FROG *Rana heckscheri*. Albert Hazen Wright identified this species in 1924 and named it after Heckscher, a noted biologist. Common names include: river-swamp frog, greenback frog, Heckscher's frog, Wright's bullfrog, and Alligator frog.

TARAHUMARA FROG *Rana tarahumarae*. In 1917, G.A. Boulenger spotted this frog in the mountainous area known as Sierra Tarahumare in northern Mexico, from which the name is derived. Common name: Mexican frog. Spanish: rana de Tarahumara.

WOOD FROG *Rana sylvatica*. In 1825, John LeConte discovered the first specimen in New York City, when there were still ample woods in the area. The frog's scientific name comes from the Latin word "sylva," meaning a woods. Common name: Cambridge frog. French Canadian: grenouille des bois.

CRICKET FROGS

The genus name *Acris* is the Greek word for locust or grasshopper. It was selected to characterize the jumping pattern of these frogs. Common names: valley cricket frog, western cricket frog, western cricket, peeper, Savanna cricket frog, rattler, sphagnum cricket frog, coastal cricket frog. Spanish: rana grillo.

NORTHERN CRICKET FROG *Acris crepitans*. Named by S.F. Baird in 1854. Crepitan is the Latin word for rattling or clattering and may have been designated to describe the vocal calls of this frog. French Canadian: rainette grillon. Spanish: rana grillo norteña.

SOUTHERN CRICKET FROG *Acris gryllus*. Named by LeConte in 1825. Gryllus is the Latin word for cricket or grasshopper.

Thomas Bewick created this wood-cut of a frog. Bewick (1753–1828) was a prominent English illustrator.

TROPICAL FROGS

Two genera are found in this category. The genus name *Eleutherodactylus* comes from a combination of Greek words, "eleutheros" for free and "dactyl" for a finger or toe. One common name for this genus is robber frogs. In Spanish, it's ranas ladrona. The genus name *Leptodactylus* comes from two Greek words, "leptos," meaning slender or thin, and "daktylos," meaning fingers. These frogs are sometimes called nest-building frogs. In Mexico, they're called ranas constructoras de nido.

BARKING FROG *Eleutherodactylus augusti*. Named in 1878 by Alfredo Dugès, who discovered the frog in Guanajuato, Mexico. The Latin word "augustus" provides the base for the species name, meaning notable. Common names: robber frog, rock frog, Texan cliff frog, and Mexican cliff frog. Spanish: rana amarilla labradora.

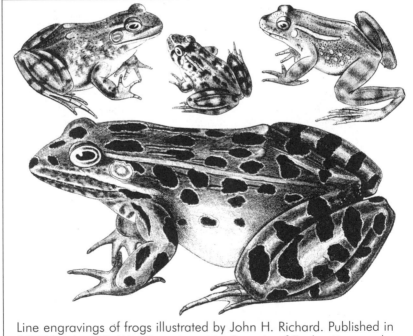

Line engravings of frogs illustrated by John H. Richard. Published in 1857 by the U.S. War Department in *Reports of Explorations and Surveys, to Ascertain the Most Practicable and Economical Route for a Railroad from the Mississippi River to the Pacific Ocean.*

CLIFF CHIRPING FROG *Eleutherodactylus marnockii*. Discovered by Cope in 1878 near San Antonio, Texas, and named for G.W. Marnock, a local herpetologist. Common name: Marnock's frog.

RIO GRANDE CHIRPING FROG *Eleutherodactylus cystignathoides*. The species name comes from two Greek words, "kystis" for pouch and "gnathos" for jaw. It was spotted and named by Cope in 1877. Spanish: ranita chirriadora del Río Bravo.

SPOTTED CHIRPING FROG *Eleutherodactylus guttilatus*. The Latin word "gutta" means having a speckled appearance. Another frog discovered by Cope, this one in 1879. Spanish: ranita de chirriadora de manchas.

WHITE-LIPPED FROG *Leptodactylus labialis*. Cope also discovered this species near Veracruz, Mexico, in 1877. The species name is a Latinized word referring to lips. Common names: white-jawed frog, white-jawed robber frog. In Mexico, it is known as ranita de charco.

TREEFROGS

Most treefrogs in North America belong to the genus *Hyla*, but there are three exceptions, the cuban treefrog, the lowland burrowing treefrog, and the Mexican treefrog, which belong to different genera (as noted in the text entries). "Hyla" is a Greek word meaning woods. In Mexico, a treefrog may be called ranita, rana arbórea, or rana arborícola. French Canadian: rainette.

BARKING TREEFROG *Hyla gratiosa*. Discovered in 1856 by LeConte. The species name comes from the Latin word "gratus," meaning pleasing. Common names: barker, coat bet, Florida treefrog, Georgia treefrog, bell frog, barking frog.

BIRD-VOICED TREEFROG *Hyla avivoca*. Percy Viosca, Jr., discovered this species in 1928 near Mandeville, Louisiana. The species name comes from two Latin words, "avis" meaning bird and "vocalis" meaning voice. At one time it was known as Hyla ogechieness, derived from the local Yuchi Indian name of the Ogeechee River. Common name: Viosca's treefrog, whistling treefrog, whistling frog.

BURROWING TREEFROG *Pternohyla fodiens*. G.A. Boulenger identified this species in 1882. The genus name comes from the Greek word "pterna," meaning heel and "Hylas," a character from Greek mythology. The species name is derived from the Latin word "fodio," meaning to dig. Spanish: ranita minera.

CALIFORNIA TREEFROG *Hyla cadaverina.* Discovered by E.D. Cope in 1866. The species name comes from the Latin word for corpse, referring to this frog's gray coloring. French Canadian: rainette de californie.

CANYON TREEFROG *Hyla arenicolor.* Described for the first time by E.D. Cope in 1866, although in 1854, Baird had earlier designated it with a Latin name that had previously been applied to a different frog. The name comes from the Latin word for the color of sand. Baird's original discovery was from the Santa Rita mountains in Arizona. Common names: canyon tree toad, desert tree toad, Arizona treefrog, Sonoran tree toad. Spanish: ranita de cañón.

CUBAN TREEFROG *Osteopilus septentrionalis.* A.M.C. Duméril and G. Bibron, French naturalists, identified this species in 1841. The species name is a Latinized word meaning of the north, chosen because the first specimen was mistakenly thought to have come from Norway. Common name: giant treefrog.

COPE'S GRAY TREEFROG *Hyla chrysoscelis.* First spotted by E.D. Cope in 1880 who named it with a Latinized word meaning gold-colored. Common names: western treefrog, northern tree toad. French-Canadian: rainette criarde.

COMMON GRAY TREEFROG *Hyla versicolor.* Identified in 1825 by John LeConte from a specimen found in New York City. The name, from the Latin, means color-turning. Common names: eastern gray treefrog, dusky tree toad, chameleon treefrog, common tree toad, common treefrog, tree toad, changeable tree toad, varying tree toad. French Canadian: rainette versicolore.

GREEN TREEFROG *Hyla cinerea.* J.G. Schneider found this frog in 1792. The name comes from the Latin word for ashes. Common names: Miller's treefrog, Carolina treefrog, marsh treefrog, cinereous frog, bell frog, fried bacon frog, cowbell frog.

MEXICAN TREEFROG *Smilisca baudinii.* In 1841, two French naturalists, A.M.C. Duméril and G. Bibron, identified this species, that they dubbed "baudini" in honor of a French commander named Baudin who provided them with the first specimen, one that he found while serving near Veracruz, Mexico. The genus name was derived from the Greek word "smile," meaning knife, with a suffix that alters it to mean little knife. Common name: Van Vliet's frog. Spanish: rana trepadora.

MOUNTAIN TREEFROG *Hyla eximia*. "Eximia" is a Latin word meaning distinguished. This frog was described for the first time by Baird in 1854 from a specimen discovered in Mexico. Spanish: ranita de montaña.

PACIFIC TREEFROG *Hyla regilla*. "Regillus" is the Latin word for regal. The Pacific treefrog was described for the first time in 1852 by Baird and Girard. Common names: wood frog, Pacific tree toad, Pacific coast tree toad. French Canadian: rainette du Pacifique.

PINE BARRENS TREEFROG *Hyla andersoni*. S.F. Baird found this frog in 1854 in South Carolina. Its Latin name commemorates Anderson, South Carolina, where the first specimen may have been discovered. Common names: Anderson treefrog, Anderson frog, green and yellow tree toad.

PINE WOODS TREEFROG *Hyla femoralis*. L.A.G. Bosc, a French naturalist, named this frog in 1800. The species name is a Latin word meaning pertaining to the thigh. Common names: pine tree toad, pine treefrog, scraper· frog, pine woods tree toad.

SQUIRREL TREEFROG *Hyla squirella*. First described in 1800 by François Daudin, a French naturalist and the author of the first major work on frogs. He found a specimen near Charleston, South Carolina. Both the common and scientific names may have come from the

Line engraving of the ornate chorus frog by T.W. Wood, a nineteenth century English illustrator.

similarity of this frog's call to that of the squirrel. Common names: southern treefrog, scraper frog, rain frog, southern tree toad, and squirrel tree toad.

CHORUS FROGS

The genus name *Pseudacris* is a combination of two words, both Greek. "Pseud" means false or deceptive — referring to the frogs' effective camouflage — and "acris," which is the Greek name for locust — referring to a similarity to the sound of this insect. For species that occur in Mexico, these frogs are called ranas de coro.

BOREAL CHORUS FROG   *Pseudacris maculata.* Identified by Luis Agassiz in 1850 and named from the Latin word "maculatus," meaning spotted.

BRIMLEY'S CHORUS FROG   *Pseudacris brimleyi.* B.B. Brandt and Charles Walker identified this species in 1933. It was named for C.S. Brimley.

LITTLE GRASS FROG   *Pseudacris ocularis.* Bosc and Daudin found this frog in 1801. The species name comes from the Latin word for eye.

MOUNTAIN CHORUS FROG   *Pseudacris brachyphona.* Cope identified this species for the first time in 1889. Common name: Ohio chorus frog.

NEW JERSEY CHORUS FROG *Pseudacris kalmi.* The species name is a Latinized word honoring Peter Kalm, a Finnish biologist who studied with Linnaeus and published *Journey to North America.* It was first identified as a separate species by F. Harper in 1955.

ORNATE CHORUS FROG *Pseudacris ornata.* In 1836, John Holbrook, a professor of anatomy and a noted herpetologist, identified this frog. The species name comes from a Latin base meaning ornate. Common names: ornate chorus frog, ornate treefrog, ornate swamp frog, swamp cricket frog, ornate winter frog, Holbrook chorus frog.

SOUTHERN CHORUS FROG *Pseudacris nigrita.* LeConte described this frog in 1825. The species name comes from the Latin root word "nigr," meaning dark or black. Common names: Florida chorus frog, Florida winter frog, striped treefrog, three-striped treefrog, swamp cricket frog, striped bush frog, three-lined treefrog, swamp treefrog, peeper, spring peeper, western striped frog, western marsh toad, spotted treefrog, peeper frog, swamp whistler, northern striped treefrog, eastern chorus frog, eastern swamp cricket frog, swamp tree toad, swamp treefrog, chorus frog, striped treefrog, common chorus frog, Clarke's chorus frog, striped chorus frog, striped treefrog, Le Conte's chorus frog, black chorus frog.

SPOTTED CHORUS FROG *Pseudacris clarki.* This species was identified by Baird in 1854 and named after Captain William Clark, half of the leadership team of the Lewis and Clark expedition. Spanish: rana de coro manchada.

SPRING PEEPER *Pseudacris crucifer.* Identified for the first time in 1838 by Maximilian Wied, from a specimen found in Leavenworth, Kansas. Common names: Florida peeper, southern peeper, Bartramian peeper, southern spring peeper, Sabalian peeper, coastal peeper, Pickering's

An illustration of frog eggs by Robert Bruce Horsfall, from the book *The Spring of the Year*, written by Dallas Lore Sharp (1912, The Riverside Press, Cambridge, Massachusetts).

treefrog, peeping frog, castanet treefrog. French Canadian: rainette crucifère.

STRECKER'S CHORUS FROG *Pseudacris streckeri*. Identified by Albert Hazen Wright and Anna Allen Wright in 1923 and named for John Strecker, a noted naturalist at Baylor University. Common names: Strecker's ornate chorus frog, Texas ornate chorus frog.

UPLAND CHORUS FROG *Pseudacris feriarum*. Named by Baird in 1854. The species name is derived from a Latin word for at rest.

WESTERN CHORUS FROG *Pseudacris triseriata*. The name is attributed to Maximilian Wied-Neuwied, who coined the name in 1838. The species name is from a Latin base and means three-striped. The first frog of this type to be named came from Posey County, Indiana. French Canadian: rainette faux-grillon de l'ouest. Common name: striped chorus frog.

SHEEP FROGS

Only one species of sheep frog is found in North America and it is called, appropriately, the sheep frog, scientific name *Hypopachus variolosus*. Cope discovered the species in 1866. The genus name comes from the Greek word for shortened and thick. The species name, from the Latin, means varied. In Spanish, it's ranas ovejeras.

TAILED FROG

The tailed frog exists as a single species in North America. The scientific name is *Ascaphus truei*. Leonhard Stejneger, a noted herpetologist at the National Museum of Natural History, first identified the tailed frog in 1899 and named it for F.W. True, the head curator of the Department of Biology at the U.S. National Museum. The genus name is from the Greek word "askaphos," meaning not digging. French Candian: grenouille-à-queue.

INTRODUCED FROGS

Foreign frogs are now at home in some parts of North America. These species have been introduced by accident, carried into the country unwittingly, or brought in deliberately as pets and exotic collectibles. Some have survived and are now considered to have self-sustaining populations.

This wood engraving from the early nineteenth century was created to be used as a graphic element in printed advertisements.

AFRICAN CLAWED FROG *Xenopus laevis*. This frog is an introduced species, brought into the country as an exotic pet to inhabit aquariums. Over time, frogs escaped — or were abandoned — in enough numbers to establish permanent populations in parts of southern California. The genus name reflects this lineage, as the word "xenos" is a Greek word meaning stranger or alien; the suffix "pus" comes from another Greek word, "podos," or foot. The species name is derived from the Latin word for smooth. Daudin is credited with first identifying this frog in 1802.

34

Illustration of African clawed frogs by M.E. Durham from *The Cambridge Natural History, Vol. VIII, Amphibia and Reptiles*, by Hans Gadow, published in 1901 by Macmillan & Company.

GREENHOUSE FROG *Eleutherodactylus planirostris*. The species name is derived from the Latin root "planos," which means roaming. The frog was first identified by Cope in 1862 and originally comes from Cuba. Spanish: rana de invernadero.

FROG SPECIES

SIZE COMPARISON

BULLFROG

NORTHERN LEOPARD FROG

WESTERN CHORUS FROG

FLORIDA LEOPARD FROG

GREEN TREEFROG

RED-LEGGED FROG

NORTHERN CRICKET FROG

LITTLE GRASS FROG

GRAY TREEFROG

CRAWFISH FROG

GREEN FROG

SPRING PEEPER

PACIFIC TREEFROG

OREGON SPOTTED FROG

PICKEREL FROG

WOOD FROG

BODY FEATURES

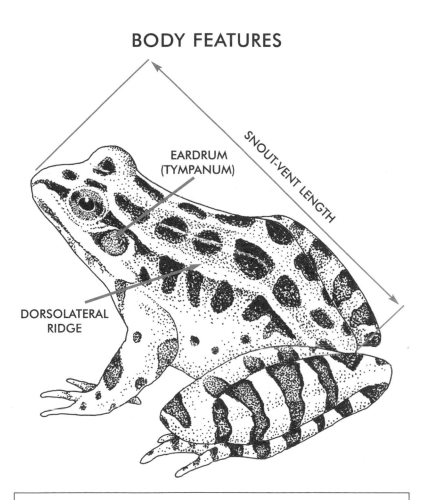

SNOUT-VENT LENGTH

EARDRUM
(TYMPANUM)

DORSOLATERAL
RIDGE

SPECIES DESCRIPTIONS NOTES

The descriptions on the following pages are based on general characteristics. Frogs of a single species can vary widely in size and coloration throughout their range as well as in the same location; a single frog may also exhibit changes in coloration at different times. The scientific names used here reflect the latest genus and species names recognized by the Society for the Study of Amphibians and Reptiles and may differ from the names used in guidebooks that have not been updated.

TRUE FROGS

NAME	Bullfrog *Rana catesbeiana*
DESCRIPTION	Largest frog in North America. Skin smooth to bumpy. Color on back green to dark green or brown to dark brown, with darker spots; lighter to white underneath; rear legs with dark banding on upper sections. Distinctive dorsolateral ridges from back of eye to back of front legs. Males smaller than females. Mostly nocturnal.
HABITAT	Lakes, ponds, streams, rivers, marshes. Prefers deep water and water cover such as aquatic vegetation.

TOTAL LENGTH	3½–8" 9–20.3 cm	VOCAL CALL	Deep, resonant call.

NAME	Carpenter frog *Rana virgatipes*
DESCRIPTION	Body brown in color with four yellow stripes running length of back; yellowish underneath with dark spots.
HABITAT	Marshes, bogs, and other wetlands. Sometimes close to slow-moving streams.

TOTAL LENGTH	1⅝–2⅝" 4.1–6.7 cm	VOCAL CALL	Repeated double note similar to sounds of a hammer.

NAME	Cascades frog *Rana cascadae*
DESCRIPTION	Color olive-green to brown on back; lighter to yellow underneath. Skin mostly smooth, folds on sides. Active during day.
HABITAT	Streams, ponds, and marshy areas.

TOTAL LENGTH	1¾–2¼" 4.4–5.7 cm	VOCAL CALL	Rapid series of low, raspy notes.

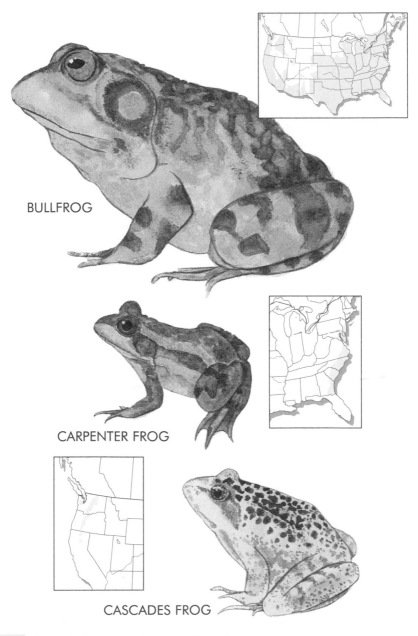

BULLFROG

CARPENTER FROG

CASCADES FROG

Approximate normal range of species

TRUE FROGS

NAME	Columbia spotted frog *Rana luteiventris*
DESCRIPTION	Color brown with irregular dark spots on back; spots may have lighter-colored centers; yellow, orange, or red underneath; may have dark mottled pattern on throat. Males smaller than females. Active day and night.
HABITAT	Streams and lakes with cold water in mountainous areas. Prefers open water with little aquatic vegetation.

TOTAL LENGTH	2–4" 5.1–10.2 cm	VOCAL CALL	Series of short croaks.

NAME	Crawfish frog *Rana areolata*
DESCRIPTION	Body short and wide. Color tan to brown or black with darker irregular markings on back and sides; pale to white underneath. Skin mostly smooth. Dorsolateral ridges present, may have yellow coloring. Mostly nocturnal.
HABITAT	Streams, ponds, marshes or other wetlands. May seek shelter in crawfish burrows or other crevices or holes along banks.

TOTAL LENGTH	2–4½" 5–11.4 cm	VOCAL CALL	Deep, resonating trill.

NAME	Florida bog frog *Rana okaloosae*
DESCRIPTION	Color yellowish green to yellowish brown; light-colored spots on lower jaw. Dorsolateral ridges present.
HABITAT	Streams, bogs, and other wetlands with shallow, non-stagnant water.

TOTAL LENGTH	about 2" 5 cm	VOCAL CALL	unavailable

COLUMBIA SPOTTED FROG

CRAWFISH FROG

FLORIDA BOG FROG

Approximate normal range of species

43

TRUE FROGS

NAME	Gopher frog *Rana capito*		
DESCRIPTION	Short body with short legs and very large head. Skin rough and warty. Color brown, reddish brown, dark gray, to black or pale with dark markings; dark-colored round spots in irregular rows on back, sides, and legs; legs may have barred pattern. Dorsolateral ridges present. Nocturnal.		
HABITAT	Ponds, streams, bogs, and other wetlands. Prefers burrows created by gopher tortoises, rodents, or crayfish.		
TOTAL LENGTH	2½–4¼" 6.4–10.8 cm	VOCAL CALL	Deep-pitched snore.

NAME	Green frog *Rana clamitans*		
DESCRIPTION	Color green to brown on back, may have darker spots and blotches; white or pale underneath with dark spots and lines; males have yellow throats. Distinctive dorsolateral ridges. Mostly nocturnal.		
HABITAT	Prefers shallow still waters and marshy areas. May be found in slow-moving shallow streams.		
TOTAL LENGTH	2–4" 5.1–10.2 cm	VOCAL CALL	One or more "twangy" notes like a loose string on a banjo.

NAME	Chiricahua leopard frog *Rana chiricahuensis*		
DESCRIPTION	Skin rough. Color green to brown; lighter to yellowish underneath; small light-colored spots on upper rear legs; may have mottled gray markings on throat and chest. Dorsolateral ridges present.		
HABITAT	Rocky streams with deep pools in oak or mixed oak woods, also streams and other wetlands, open grasslands and desert.		
TOTAL LENGTH	2–5½" 5.1–13.9 cm	VOCAL CALL	Single snoring note lasting 1–2 seconds, dropping in pitch.

GOPHER FROG

GREEN FROG

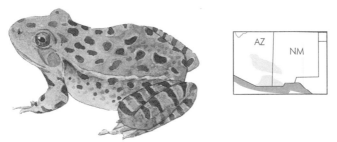

CHIRICAHUA LEOPARD FROG

Approximate normal range of species

45

TRUE FROGS

NAME	Florida leopard frog *Rana sphenocephala*
DESCRIPTION	Slender body with narrow head. Color green to brown with large dark spots on back; light-colored stripe on upper jaw; may have a light-colored spot centered in the eardrum. Dorsolateral ridges present. Mostly nocturnal.
HABITAT	Streams, ponds, marshes, and other wetlands. Can be found in both fresh and brackish water.

TOTAL LENGTH	2–5" 5.1–12.7 cm	VOCAL CALL	Series of short, gruff croaks.

NAME	Lowland leopard frog *Rana yavapaiensis*
DESCRIPTION	Skin smooth. Color light brown, pale grayish-green, grayish brown, or green with darker markings on back; yellow underneath; upper rear legs have dark-colored pattern. Dorsolateral ridges present.
HABITAT	Streams with permanent pools, springs, and other wetlands in oak or mixed oak woods, desert, or prairie.

TOTAL LENGTH	about 5½" 14 cm	VOCAL CALL	unavailable

NAME	Northern leopard frog *Rana pipiens*
DESCRIPTION	Body narrow. Color brown or green with large dark spots on back, spots may have lighter-colored edges; paler underneath; light-colored stripe on upper jaw. Dorsolateral ridges reach to rear and are lighter in color. Mostly nocturnal.
HABITAT	Ponds, streams, and other wetlands. Also found in damp meadows and other wet grassy areas away from water.

TOTAL LENGTH	2–5" 5.1–12.7 cm	VOCAL CALL	Deep rattling "snore" broken with single "clucking" notes.

FLORIDA LEOPARD FROG

LOWLAND LEOPARD FROG

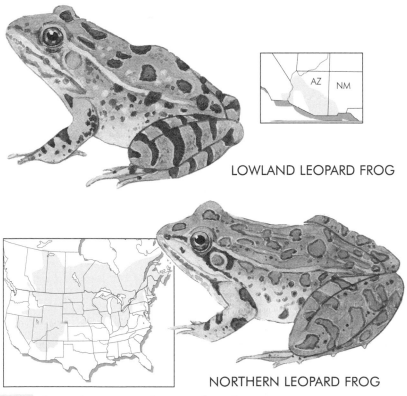

NORTHERN LEOPARD FROG

Approximate normal range of species

47

TRUE FROGS

NAME	Plains leopard frog *Rana blairi*		
DESCRIPTION	Body wide. Color green to brown with large dark spots on back; belly and underside of upper legs yellow; distinctive light-colored stripe on upper jaw. Dorsolateral ridges end before hind legs; may be yellowish in color. Mostly nocturnal.		
HABITAT	Open, grassy areas near running or still water or other wetlands.		
TOTAL LENGTH	2–4¼" 5.1–10.8 cm	VOCAL CALL	Series of guttural "chucks" at rate of 2 to 3 per second.

NAME	Ramsey Canyon leopard frog *Rana subaquavocalis*		
DESCRIPTION	Large body. Color green with large dark spots, may have lighter-colored edges. Dorsolateral ridges lighter in color. Extremely rare.		
HABITAT	Streams and ponds from 5,000–6,000 feet.		
TOTAL LENGTH	6–8" 15.2–20.3 cm	VOCAL CALL	Mating calls made while submerged.

NAME	Relict leopard frog *Rana onca*		
DESCRIPTION	Body narrow. Color brown with large dark spots, which may have lighter-colored edges; lighter-colored stripe on upper jaw. Dorsolateral ridges may be light in color. Mostly nocturnal.		
HABITAT	Ponds, marshes, and other wetlands.		
TOTAL LENGTH	1¾–3⅜" 4.4–8.4 cm	VOCAL CALL	Low rumbling "snore."

PLAINS LEOPARD FROG

RAMSEY CANYON LEOPARD FROG

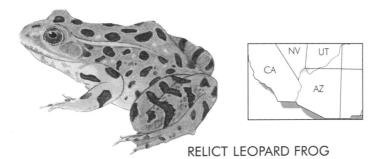

RELICT LEOPARD FROG

Approximate normal range of species

49

NAME	Rio Grande leopard frog *Rana berlandieri*
DESCRIPTION	Skin smooth. Color light brown to green with irregular rows of large dark spots on back, spots bordered in lighter color; light-colored stripe on upper jaw. Dorsolateral ridges present. Mostly nocturnal.
HABITAT	Streams, ponds, and other wetlands in dry regions.

TOTAL LENGTH	2¼–4½" 5.7–11.4 cm	VOCAL CALL	Deep-pitched rapid trill of short duration, repeated.

NAME	Maslin's wood frog *Rana maslini*
DESCRIPTION	Color pinkish to dark brown; white underneath, may have dark mottled pattern; distinctive dark mask on sides of face; dark-colored marks near top of front legs; lighter-colored stripe on upper jaw. Dorsolateral ridges present. Active mostly during day.
HABITAT	Wetlands, damp woods, and open plains near water sources.

TOTAL LENGTH	1¼–3¼" 3.2–8.3 cm	VOCAL CALL	Series of short, quack-like notes.

NAME	Mink frog *Rana septentrionalis*
DESCRIPTION	Color olive-green to brown on back with dark spots and irregular markings; pale to yellowish underneath. May have visible dorsolateral ridges. Distinctive musky odor. Mostly nocturnal.
HABITAT	Still and running water, prefers water lily pads or other dense aquatic vegetation.

TOTAL LENGTH	1¾–3" 4.5–7.6 cm	VOCAL CALL	Series of deep, rough notes.

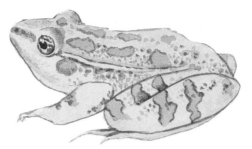

RIO GRANDE LEOPARD FROG

MASLIN'S WOOD FROG

MINK FROG

Approximate normal range of species

NAME	Oregon spotted frog *Rana pretiosa*
DESCRIPTION	Color brown with irregular dark spots on back; spots may have lighter-colored centers; yellow, orange, or red underneath; may have dark mottled pattern on throat. Males smaller than females. Active day and night.
HABITAT	Streams and lakes with cold water in mountainous areas. Prefers open water with little aquatic vegetation.

TOTAL LENGTH	2–4" 5.1–10.2 cm	VOCAL CALL	Series of short croaks.

NAME	Pickerel frog *Rana palustris*
DESCRIPTION	Color tannish brown, large dark irregular markings — somewhat squarish in shape — run in parallel rows along back; yellow to orange underneath and on bottom of back legs; lighter-colored stripe on upper jaw. Dorsolateral ridges yellow in color. Nocturnal.
HABITAT	Slow-moving streams, ponds, marshes and other wetlands. Prefers areas with low, dense vegetation.

TOTAL LENGTH	1¾–3½" 4.5–8.9 cm	VOCAL CALL	Deep "snoring" note lasting 1 to 2 seconds.

NAME	Pig frog *Rana grylio*
DESCRIPTION	Large body with small, pointed head. Color olive-green to brown with dark spots; cream-colored underneath; may have band of darker color or spots on upper legs. Nocturnal. Spends most of the time in the water.
HABITAT	Ponds, streams, marshes and other wetlands. Prefers dense aquatic vegetation.

TOTAL LENGTH	3¼–6½" 8.3–16.5 cm	VOCAL CALL	Short, grunt-like note.

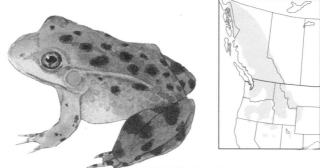

OREGON SPOTTED FROG

PICKEREL FROG

PIG FROG

Approximate normal range of species

53

NAME	Red-legged frog *Rana aurora*
DESCRIPTION	Body large with prominent head. Color reddish-brown to gray with darker spots and irregular markings; yellow underneath with reddish tinge on lower belly and under hind legs; may have darker-colored mask on head; lighter-colored stripe on upper jaw. Prominent dorsolateral ridges. Active mostly during day.
HABITAT	Ponds and streams with dense vegetation or damp woods.

TOTAL LENGTH	2–5¼" 5.1–13.3 cm	VOCAL CALL	Series of thin, rough notes.

NAME	River frog *Rana heckscheri*
DESCRIPTION	Large body with rough skin. Color green to greenish-black; darker underneath with dark spots and irregular lines; distinctive light-colored spots around jaws. Nocturnal.
HABITAT	Wetlands near ponds and slow-moving streams and rivers.

TOTAL LENGTH	3¼–5¼" 8.3–13.3 cm	VOCAL CALL	Deep prolonged "snoring" note or short grunt.

NAME	Tarahumara frog *Rana tarahumarae*
DESCRIPTION	Body large and wide. Color olive-green to brown with dark spots; white to cream-colored underneath; darker banding pattern on rear legs. Nocturnal.
HABITAT	Pools and streams in canyons between elevations of 1500 and 6000 feet (457–1829 m).

TOTAL LENGTH	2¼–4½" 5.4–11.4 cm	VOCAL CALL	Does not vocalize.

RED-LEGGED FROG

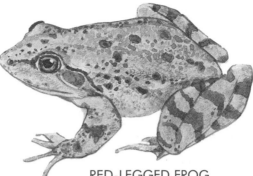

RIVER FROG

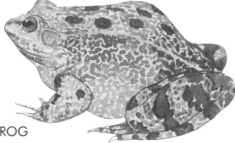

TARAHUMARA FROG

Approximate normal range of species

TRUE FROGS

NAME	Foothill yellow-legged frog *Rana boylei*
DESCRIPTION	Color gray or brown to olive-green, may have darker irregular markings on back; yellow on lower belly and underside of legs; may have lighter-colored band on top of head; may have darker-colored bands on front and rear legs. Active mostly during day.
HABITAT	Streams with open banks, elevations from sea level up to 6000 feet (1829 m).

TOTAL LENGTH	1½–3" 3.8–7.6 cm	VOCAL CALL	Series or rapid, rasping notes.

NAME	Mountain yellow-legged frog *Rana muscosa*
DESCRIPTION	Color brown with darker spots and markings in lichen-like patterns; yellow to light orange underneath. May have visible dorsolateral ridges. Musky odor. Active mostly during day.
HABITAT	Ponds, lakes, and streams at elevations of 1200 to 12000 feet (366–3658 m). Prefers aquatic habitat with gravel banks.

TOTAL LENGTH	2–3¼" 5.1–8.3 cm	VOCAL CALL	Does not vocalize.

NAME	Wood frog *Rana sylvatica*
DESCRIPTION	Color pinkish to dark brown; white underneath, may have dark mottled pattern; distinctive dark mask on sides of face; dark-colored marks near top of front legs; lighter-colored stripe on upper jaw. Dorsolateral ridges present. Active mostly during day.
HABITAT	Wetlands, damp woods, and open plains near water sources.

TOTAL LENGTH	1¼–3¼" 3.2–8.3 cm	VOCAL CALL	Series of short, quack-like notes.

FOOTHILL YELLOW-LEGGED FROG

MOUNTAIN YELLOW-LEGGED FROG

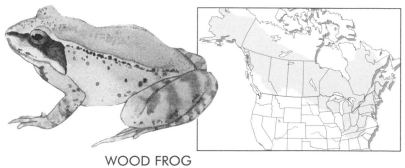

WOOD FROG

Approximate normal range of species

CRICKET FROGS

NAME	Northern cricket frog *Acris crepitans*
DESCRIPTION	Short, blunt head shape with rounded nose. Skin rough. Color greenish-brown to black, yellow, or red, may have darker markings and stripes on back; dark stripes with ragged edges on back of upper legs; may have distinctive dark triangle marking between eyes. Active during day.
HABITAT	Slow-moving streams and shallow ponds with dense aquatic vegetation. Prefers open areas with sunshine.

TOTAL LENGTH	⅝ – 1½" 1.6–3.8 cm	VOCAL CALL	High, rhythmic clicking.

NAME	Southern cricket frog *Acris gryllus*
DESCRIPTION	Head with pointed nose. Rough skin. Color green, brown to black, or red; dark stripes across back of upper legs; may have distinctive dark triangular patch between eyes. Active during the day.
HABITAT	Ponds, lakes, streams, marshes, and other wetlands.

TOTAL LENGTH	⅝ – 1¼" 1.6–3.2 cm	VOCAL CALL	Series of rapid metallic "click-click" notes.

NORTHERN CRICKET FROG

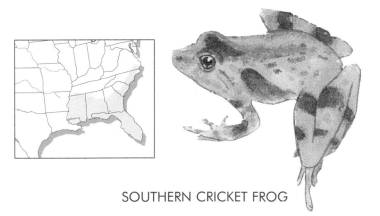

SOUTHERN CRICKET FROG

Approximate normal range of species

NAME	Barking frog *Eleutherodactylus augusti*
DESCRIPTION	Body wide and squat like that of a toad; large head. Skin smooth. Color green to light brown with dark spots; lighter underneath. Dorsolateral folds on sides; fold at back of head. Nocturnal.
HABITAT	Damp holes, crevices, and caves. Prefers limestone surfaces.

TOTAL LENGTH	2½–3¾" 6.4–9.5 cm	VOCAL CALL	Sharp "barking" note.

NAME	Cliff chirping frog *Eleutherodactylus marnockii*
DESCRIPTION	Body somewhat flattened in shape; large head. Skin smooth. Color green with dark mottled markings; lighter underneath. Mostly nocturnal.
HABITAT	Holes, crevices, and caves in limestone outcroppings.

TOTAL LENGTH	¾–1½" 1.9–3.8 cm	VOCAL CALL	Cricket-like chirping.

NAME	Rio Grande chirping frog *Eleutherodactylus cystignathoides*
DESCRIPTION	Smooth skin. Color grayish-yellow to brown with slightly darker markings; lighter underneath. Nocturnal.
HABITAT	Thickets, wetlands, lawns, and damp ground with shade and covering vegetation.

TOTAL LENGTH	⅝–1" 1.6–2.5 cm	VOCAL CALL	Soft, short cricket-like chirping.

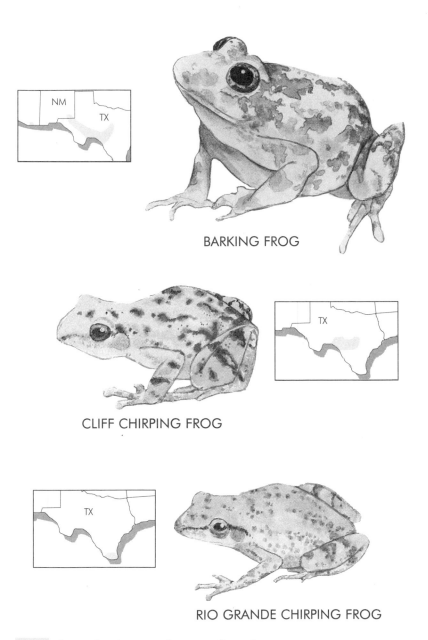

BARKING FROG

CLIFF CHIRPING FROG

RIO GRANDE CHIRPING FROG

Approximate normal range of species

NAME	Spotted chirping frog *Eleutherodactylus guttilatus*
DESCRIPTION	Skin smooth. Color yellowish-brown to brown with dark markings. Nocturnal.
HABITAT	Springs, streams, and damp caves.

TOTAL LENGTH	¾–1¼" 1.9–3.2 cm	VOCAL CALL	Short single notes.

NAME	White-lipped frog *Leptodactylus labialis*
DESCRIPTION	Color gray to brown with dark spots on back; lighter underneath; distinctive lighter stripe on upper jaw; dark irregular striping on rear legs. Dorsolateral ridges on sides.
HABITAT	Damp meadows, fields, and open areas and other wetlands.

TOTAL LENGTH	1⅜–2" 2.9–5.1 cm	VOCAL CALL	Double note with second note higher in pitch.

NAME	Greenhouse frog *Eleutherodactylus planirostris*
DESCRIPTION	Skin rough. Color brown to reddish-brown with dark markings or light-colored stripes on back; white underneath with delicate dark markings. Nocturnal. Non-native, introduced accidentally from Cuba.
HABITAT	Damp, sheltered groundcover on lawns, gardens, meadows, streams, marshes, and other wetlands.

TOTAL LENGTH	⅝–1¼" 1.6–3.2 cm	VOCAL CALL	Repeated musical note like a bird call.

SPOTTED CHIRPING FROG

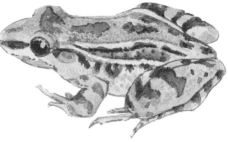

WHITE-LIPPED FROG

GREENHOUSE FROG

Approximate normal range of species

NAME	Barking treefrog *Hyla gratiosa*		
DESCRIPTION	One of the largest treefrogs. Body wide. Skin rough. Color bright green to dark brown, pale gray or yellow, may have dark spots; lighter underneath; lighter stripes on sides; yellow to green throat on males. Nocturnal.		
HABITAT	Treetops during warm months; may hide in vegetation close to the ground or burrow in tree roots at other times.		
TOTAL LENGTH	2–2¾" 5.1–7 cm	VOCAL CALL	Series of barking notes; mating call is single resonant note.

NAME	Bird-voiced treefrog *Hyla avivoca*		
DESCRIPTION	Green, gray, or brown with dark irregular markings on back; spots under eyes have dark edges; underside of hind legs pale yellow-green to yellowish-white. Nocturnal.		
HABITAT	Streams, rivers, and wetlands with heavy wooded areas.		
TOTAL LENGTH	1⅛–2⅛" 2.7–5.2 cm	VOCAL CALL	Series of short, bird-like whistles.

NAME	California treefrog *Hyla cadaverina*		
DESCRIPTION	Skin rough. Color gray with dark irregular markings; gray throat on males. Mostly nocturnal.		
HABITAT	Slow-moving streams and ponds at elevations from sea level to 5,000 feet (1523 m).		
TOTAL LENGTH	1–2" 2.5–5.1 cm	VOCAL CALL	Deep, short quack-like note.

BARKING TREEFROG

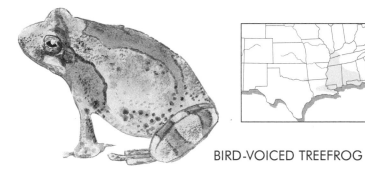

BIRD-VOICED TREEFROG

CALIFORNIA TREEFROG

Approximate normal range of species

TREEFROGS

NAME	Canyon treefrog *Hyla arenicolor*
DESCRIPTION	Body wide and toad-like. Skin rough and warty. Color olive-green to brownish-gray with dark irregular markings on back; light-colored spot with dark edge below eyes; underside of upper hind legs yellow or orange; gray to black throats on males. Mostly nocturnal.
HABITAT	Small pools and streams in rocky, arid canyons.

TOTAL LENGTH	1¼–2¼" 3.2–5.7 cm	VOCAL CALL	Series of short nasal notes.

NAME	Cope's gray treefrog *Hyla chrysoscelis*
DESCRIPTION	Skin rough. Color gray to greenish-gray with dark irregular markings on back; lighter underneath; light-colored spot with dark edge under eyes; underside of upper hind legs bright gold, yellow, or orange with dark mottled pattern. Nocturnal. Identical in appearance to gray treefrog except for vocal calls.
HABITAT	Trees and shrubbery close to ponds, lakes, streams, and other wetlands.

TOTAL LENGTH	1¼–2¼" 3.2–5.7 cm	VOCAL CALL	High, fast musical trill.

NAME	Gray treefrog *Hyla versicolor*
DESCRIPTION	Skin rough. Color gray to greenish-gray with dark irregular markings on back; lighter underneath; light-colored spot with dark edge under eyes; underside of upper hind legs bright gold, yellow, or orange with dark mottled pattern. Nocturnal. Identical in appearance to Cope's gray treefrog except for vocal calls.
HABITAT	Trees and shrubbery close to ponds, lakes, streams, and other wetlands.

TOTAL LENGTH	1¼–2¼" 3.2–5.7 cm	VOCAL CALL	High, slow musical trill.

CANYON TREEFROG

COPE'S GRAY TREEFROG

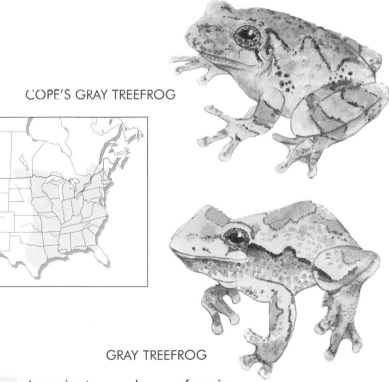

GRAY TREEFROG

Approximate normal range of species

NAME	Green treefrog *Hyla cinerea*
DESCRIPTION	Color bright green, yellow, or slate-gray, may have small gold spots with dark edges on back; distinctive light-colored stripe on upper jaw; may have light-colored stripe along sides of body.
HABITAT	Ponds, lakes, marshes, and other wetlands or damp areas near permanent bodies of water.

TOTAL LENGTH	1¼–2½" 3.2–6.4 cm	VOCAL CALL	Ringing bell-like notes.

NAME	Mountain treefrog *Hyla eximia*
DESCRIPTION	Skin smooth. Color green, light brown, or black, may have a few dark irregular markings on lower back; lighter underneath; dark stripe with light-colored edge runs from nose along sides of body to rear; olive-green throat on males. Nocturnal.
HABITAT	Slow-moving streams and pools in forested areas at elevations above 5,000 feet (1523 m).

TOTAL LENGTH	¾–2¼" 1.9–5.7 cm	VOCAL CALL	Series of low, rough metallic notes at rate of 2–3 per second.

NAME	Pacific treefrog *Hyla regilla*
DESCRIPTION	Skin rough. Color green, light brown, or black, may have dark spots or irregular markings; lighter underneath; distinctive dark stripe extends from nose through eyes and along sides of head; may have dark triangular marking between eyes; gray throat on males. Active during night and daytime periods.
HABITAT	Grassy or shrubby areas close to ponds and streams at elevations from sea level to 10,000 feet (3,046 m).

TOTAL LENGTH	¾–2" 1.9–5.1 cm	VOCAL CALL	High, double note.

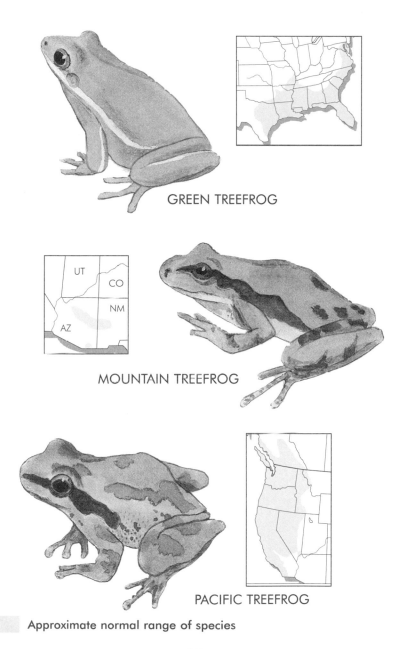

GREEN TREEFROG

UT
CO
NM
AZ

MOUNTAIN TREEFROG

PACIFIC TREEFROG

Approximate normal range of species

NAME	Pine barrens treefrog *Hyla andersoni*
DESCRIPTION	Color bright green; lavender stripes with light-colored edges run from nose through eyes and along sides; underside of rear legs orange. Nocturnal.
HABITAT	Streams, marshes, and other wetlands. Prefers acidic bogs.
TOTAL LENGTH	1⅛–2" 2.9–5.1 cm	VOCAL CALL	Series of low nasal "honking" notes at rate of 1 per second.

NAME	Pine woods treefrog *Hyla femoralis*
DESCRIPTION	Color gray, greenish-gray, or reddish-brown, may have dark irregular markings on back; white to yellow spots on underside of rear legs. Nocturnal.
HABITAT	Pine forests near streams, ponds, marshes, or other wetlands.
TOTAL LENGTH	1–1¾" 2.5–4.5 cm	VOCAL CALL	Series of Morse-code-like notes.

NAME	Squirrel treefrog *Hyla squirella*
DESCRIPTION	Color green to brown, may have dark or gold spots on back; may have dark stripe between eyes; may have light-colored stripe along sides. Nocturnal.
HABITAT	Wide range of damp cover, including forests, shrubbery, and lawns.
TOTAL LENGTH	⅞–1⅝" 2.2–4.1 cm	VOCAL CALL	Notes similar to scolding squirrel; mating call nasal trill.

PINE BARRENS TREEFROG

PINE WOODS TREEFROG

SQUIRREL TREEFROG

Approximate normal range of species

71

OTHER TREEFROGS

NAME	Cuban treefrog *Osteopilus septentrionalis*
DESCRIPTION	Largest treefrog in North America. Skin rough and warty. Color green to gray with slightly darker irregular markings; lighter underneath. Females larger than males. Nocturnal. Non-native species, introduced from Cuba.
HABITAT	Damp cover in shady areas, especially around trees and shrubs.

TOTAL LENGTH	1½–5½" 3.8–14 cm	VOCAL CALL	Raspy "snoring" note that varies in pitch.

NAME	Lowland burrowing treefrog *Pternohyla fodiens*
DESCRIPTION	Body wide and squat like toad. Color pale yellow to brown with large distinctive dark markings or stripes, edged with black; lighter underneath; gray throat on males. Distinctive skin fold behind head. Nocturnal.
HABITAT	Meadows and other grassy areas and open mesquite forests at elevations from sea level to 5,000 feet (1,522 m).

TOTAL LENGTH	1–2" 2.5–5.1 cm	VOCAL CALL	Series of loud, deep croaks.

NAME	Mexican treefrog *Smilisca baudinii*
DESCRIPTION	Color light green to dark green, yellow, or gray, may have darker markings on back; lighter underneath; light-colored spot with dark edge under eyes; may have dark-colored streak running from nose through eye and onto shoulders. Nocturnal.
HABITAT	Trees and shrubs in damp areas near streams and pools in canyons at elevations from sea level to 3,300 feet (1,005 m).

TOTAL LENGTH	2–3⅝" 5.1–9.2 cm	VOCAL CALL	Series of short, explosive notes.

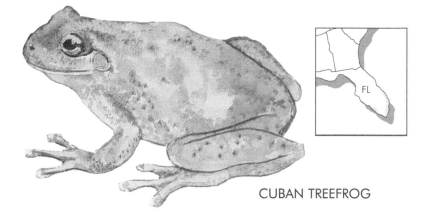

CUBAN TREEFROG

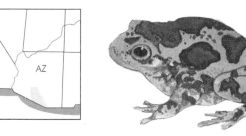

LOWLAND BURROWING TREEFROG

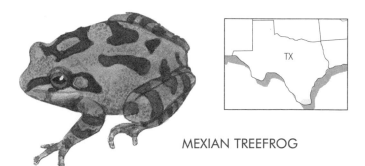

MEXIAN TREEFROG

Approximate normal range of species

NAME	Boreal chorus frog *Pseudacris maculata*
DESCRIPTION	Body narrow with short legs. Skin smooth. Color greenish-brown to brown with several dark irregular stripes on back, may have dark spots; lighter underneath; dark-colored stripe from nose through eye and along sides of head. Nocturnal.
HABITAT	Streams, ponds, and marshes in mountainous areas.

TOTAL LENGTH	¾–1½" 1.9–3.8 cm	VOCAL CALL	Serrated note like plucking teeth of a comb.

NAME	Brimley's chorus frog *Pseudacris brimleyi*
DESCRIPTION	Body slender. Skin slightly rough. Color light brown to yellowish-brown with three dark stripes on back; dark spots on chest; lighter to yellowish underneath; distinctive dark-colored stripe from nose along sides of body. Mostly nocturnal.
HABITAT	Marshes and other wetlands and damp open forests with sparse vegetation.

TOTAL LENGTH	1–1¼" 2.5–3.2 cm	VOCAL CALL	Series of short, single raspy trilled notes.

NAME	Illinois chorus frog *Pseudacris illinoensis*
DESCRIPTION	Body wide and toad-like. Color green to reddish-brown or gray, may have large dark irregular markings on back; lighter underneath; distinctive dark stripe from nose through eyes and along sides, breaking up into pale spots; may have dark spot below eyes. Nocturnal.
HABITAT	Damp areas in woods, fields, marshes, or other wetlands.

TOTAL LENGTH	1–1¾" 2.5–4.5 cm	VOCAL CALL	Single, bell-like note.

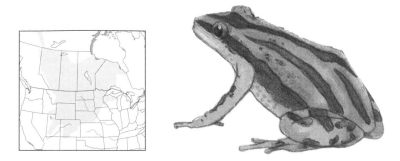

BOREAL CHORUS FROG

BRIMLEY'S CHORUS FROG

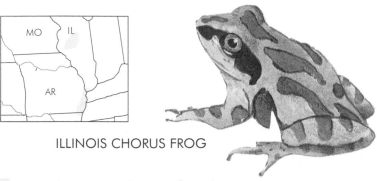

ILLINOIS CHORUS FROG

Approximate normal range of species

75

CHORUS FROGS

NAME	Little grass frog *Pseudacris ocularis*
DESCRIPTION	Smallest frog in North America. Skin smooth. Color light brown to greenish-gray, may have dark stripe down back; white to yellowish on chest and underneath; dark-colored stripe from nose through eye and along sides. Mostly nocturnal.
HABITAT	Damp, grassy areas next to ponds, streams, ditches, bays, and other wetlands.

TOTAL LENGTH	$^1/_2$–$^5/_8$" 1.3–1.6 cm	VOCAL CALL	High, thin "tinkling" notes similar to insect calls.

NAME	Mountain chorus frog *Pseudacris brachyphona*
DESCRIPTION	Skin slightly rough. Color green to olive-green to brown with two dark curving stripes (sometimes in the shape of parenthesis marks) which may overlap; lighter to yellowish underneath; dark-colored stripe from nose through eye and along sides; may have dark triangular-shaped mark between eyes. Mostly nocturnal.
HABITAT	Forested areas in hilly terrain, sometimes far from sources of water. Elevations up to 3,500 feet (1,066 m).

TOTAL LENGTH	1–1½" 2.5–3.8 cm	VOCAL CALL	Series of high squeaky notes.

NAME	New Jersey chorus frog *Pseudacris kalmi*
DESCRIPTION	Skin smooth. Color greenish-gray, brown to gray, with three dark stripes or series of spots in three lines on back; cream-colored underneath, may have dark markings on chest; dark-colored stripe from nose through eye and along sides; light-colored stripe on upper jaw. Nocturnal.
HABITAT	Forested areas, marshes, and grassy areas in a variety of dry to wet habitats.

TOTAL LENGTH	¾–1½" 1.9–3.8 cm	VOCAL CALL	Rasping trill, rising in pitch.

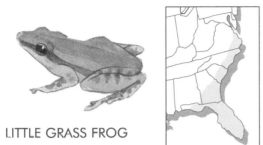

LITTLE GRASS FROG

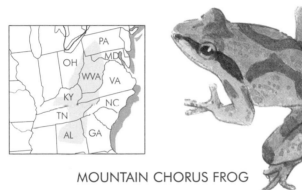

MOUNTAIN CHORUS FROG

NEW JERSEY CHORUS FROG

Approximate normal range of species

77

CHORUS FROGS

NAME	Ornate chorus frog *Pseudacris ornata*		
DESCRIPTION	Body wide. Color reddish-brown, light brown, almost white, green, or blackish with a few dark irregular markings on back; distinctive large dark spots on sides; pale to yellowish underneath; dark-colored stripe from nose through eye and along sides. Nocturnal.		
HABITAT	Ponds, flooded meadows, and other wetlands with shallow water and sparse vegetation.		
TOTAL LENGTH	1–1¼" 2.5–3.2 cm	VOCAL CALL	Series of single high metallic notes at rate of 1 per second.

NAME	Southern chorus frog *Pseudacris nigrita*		
DESCRIPTION	Skin rough and warty. Color light brown to gray with three dark stripes or rows of spots on back; lighter underneath; dark-colored stripe from nose through eye and along sides of body; may have light-colored stripe on upper jaw. Mostly nocturnal.		
HABITAT	Damp forests, meadows, streams, ditches, and other wetlands.		
TOTAL LENGTH	¾–1¼" 1.9–3.2 cm	VOCAL CALL	Raspy musical trill.

NAME	Spotted chorus frog *Pseudacris clarki*		
DESCRIPTION	Color light gray to olive-gray with green irregular markings edged with black, markings may be formed into stripes; lighter to white underneath; green stripe runs from nose through eye and along sides; may have green triangular marking between eyes. Nocturnal.		
HABITAT	Open grasslands.		
TOTAL LENGTH	¾–1¼" 1.9–3.2 cm	VOCAL CALL	Series of raspy trills like the sound of a saw.

ORNATE CHORUS FROG

SOUTHERN CHORUS FROG

SPOTTED CHORUS FROG

Approximate normal range of species

NAME	Spring peeper *Pseudacris crucifer*
DESCRIPTION	Color brown or tan to gray with dark marking in form of stripes or the figure "X" on back; white to yellowish underneath; yellowish or pinkish on underside of rear legs and groin; rear legs may have darker crossbar markings. Males usually slightly smaller and darker than females. Nocturnal.
HABITAT	Forested areas near streams, ponds, and marshes.

TOTAL LENGTH	¾–1½" 1.9–3.8 cm	VOCAL CALL	High-pitched peep once every second or two.

NAME	Strecker's chorus frog *Pseudacris streckeri*
DESCRIPTION	Body wide and toad-like. Color green to reddish-brown or gray, may have large dark irregular markings on back; lighter underneath; distinctive dark stripe from nose through eyes and along sides, breaking up into spots; may have dark spot below eyes. Nocturnal.
HABITAT	Damp forested areas, grassy areas and meadows, fields, streams, ponds, marshes, and other wetlands.

TOTAL LENGTH	1–1¾" 2.5–4.5 cm	VOCAL CALL	Single bell-like note.

NAME	Upland chorus frog *Pseudacris feriarum*
DESCRIPTION	Color brown to gray, may have three dark stripes or series of spots on back; cream-colored underneath, may have dark markings on chest; dark-colored stripe from nose through eyes and along sides; light-colored stripe on upper jaw. Nocturnal.
HABITAT	Grassy areas, damp forests, streams, ponds, marshes, and other wetlands.

TOTAL LENGTH	¾–1½" 1.9–3.8 cm	VOCAL CALL	Repeated raspy trill.

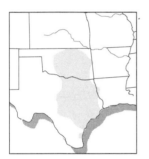

SPRING PEEPER

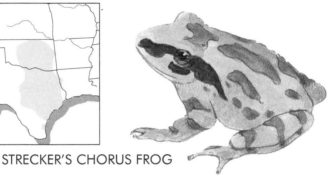

STRECKER'S CHORUS FROG

UPLAND CHORUS FROG

Approximate normal range of species

81

NAME	Western chorus frog *Pseudacris triseriata*
DESCRIPTION	Color light gray to dark brown, green to olive-green, with three dark stripes on back; lighter to white underneath; dark-colored stripe from nose through eyes and along sides; may have dark-colored triangular marking between eyes; light-colored stripe on upper jaw. Nocturnal.
HABITAT	Wet and dry habitats from woodlands to prairies, including agricultural areas and urban settings.

TOTAL LENGTH	¾–1½" 1.9–3.8 cm	VOCAL CALL	Raspy trill, rising in pitch, like sound of plucked comb.

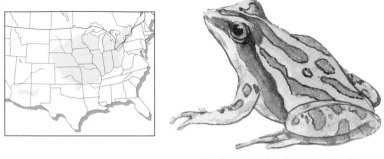

WESTERN CHORUS FROG

Approximate normal range of species

NAME	Sheep frog *Hypopachus variolosus*		
DESCRIPTION	Body wide and toad-like with small, pointed head. Skin smooth. Color olive-green to brown with distinctive thin yellowish stripe in center of back, may have dark spots and markings; lighter to gray underneath with darker markings and light-colored line in center of belly; dark-colored throat in males. Fold on back of head. Nocturnal.		
HABITAT	Streams, ponds, and marshes in dry areas.		
TOTAL LENGTH	1–1¾" 2.5–4.5 cm	VOCAL CALL	Single sheep-like bleat about 2 seconds in duration.

NAME	Tailed frog *Ascaphus truei*		
DESCRIPTION	Skin rough. Color olive-green to almost black with numerous dark spots on back; may have dark-colored stripe from nose through eyes and along sides; yellowish triangular marking on nose. Distinctive tail-like appendage on males.		
HABITAT	Cold water streams and damp forests in mountainous terrain.		
TOTAL LENGTH	1–2" 2.5–5.1 cm	VOCAL CALL	Does not vocalize.

NAME	African clawed frog *Xenopus laevis*		
DESCRIPTION	Body large with small pointed head. Color greenish-brown to gray with dark markings; lighter to white underneath. Males smaller than females. Nocturnal. Not native to North America, introduced as aquarium pets and now part of permanent populations in limited areas.		
HABITAT	Slow-moving streams, ponds, marshes, and other wetlands.		
TOTAL LENGTH	2–3¾" 5.1–9.5 cm	VOCAL CALL	Loud rattling note.

84

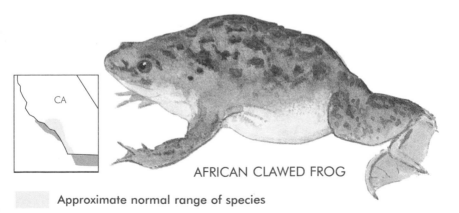
SHEEP FROG

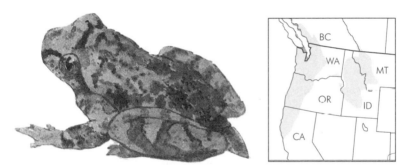
TAILED FROG

AFRICAN CLAWED FROG

Approximate normal range of species

85

EVOLUTION

"If tree-frogs were of great rarity and inhabited only one remote island of a far-distant archipelago, their arboreal habits would be accounted as much of a wonder as the flying-frog of Borneo."

— William T. Hornaday
(*Hornaday's American Natural History*, 1927)

The frogs we are familiar with in the modern world are the latest stage in a chain of development that has been traced back as far as the Devonian period, about 400 million years ago. During that ancient era the first known amphibians, known as labryinthodonts, emerged from the water to spend part or all of their lives on land. From this beginning came further changes that gradually turned them into frog-like animals. The first known fossils of animals that we recognize as frog-like date to the early Jurassic period, between 188 and 213 million years ago, before most of the major types of dinosaurs had emerged. These animals are sometimes called "proto-frogs" because some, though not all, frog-like features were present.

At some point, the amphibians divided into three major groups, forming the three orders that comprise amphibians alive today: the Apoda, footless, worm-like animals that are found in tropical areas; the Caudata, salamanders and newts; and the Anura, or anurans, frogs and toads.

Frogs and toads pose puzzling problems for the scientists who attempt to organize them into distinct groups. Among many species, some physical similarities hide significant genetic differences and some physical differences belie significant genetic similarities. Also, as more and more of the remote areas of the world are explored in depth by biologists, new species are continually being discovered. As a current estimate, there are more than 4,500 species of frogs and toads worldwide. In North America, by the latest count, there are 95 species of frogs and toads, divided among 16 genera. In general,

WORLD FROGS AND TOADS

FAMILY	DESCRIPTION	No. of GENERA	No. of SPECIES
BRACHYCEPHALIDAE	Brazilian terrestrial toads	2	2
BUFONIDAE	true toads	25	335
CENTROLENIDAE	leaf frogs	2	65
DENDROBATIDAE	dart-poison frogs	4	117
DISCOGLOSSIDAE	fire-bellied toads, midwife toads	5	14
HELEOPHRYNIDAE	South African mountain frogs	1	3
HYLIDAE	treefrogs	37	630
HYPEROLIIDAE	African treefrogs	14	206
LEIOPELMATIDAE	primitive frogs	2	4
LEPTODACTYLIDAE	tropical frogs	51	710
MICROHYLIDAE	narrow-mouthed toads	61	279
MYOBATRACHIDAE	terrestrial, arboreal, and aquatic frogs	20	99
PELOBATIDEA	spadefoot toads	9	83
PELODYTIDAE	spadefoot toads	1	2
PIPIDAE	tongueless frogs	4	26
PSEUDIDAE	aquatic frogs	2	4
RANIDAE	true frogs	47	667
RHACOPHORIDAE	old world tropical frogs	10	186
RHINODERMATIDAE	mouth-breeding frog	1	2
RHINOPHRYNIDAE	burrowing toad	1	1
SOOGLOSSIDAE	terrestrial frogs	2	3

NOTE: This list is derived from recent classification information based on work by D. Frost. Other classification schemes shift some genera from one family to another or combine certain families into larger groups. No classification scheme should be considered final. Also, as new species are likely to be recognized during ongoing research, this list is only a temporary guide.

the hotter and more tropical the local climate, the greater the number of species.

In a single valley in the Ecuadoran region of the Amazon, for example, there are more than 80 species. Frogs live at all elevations, from sea level to 12,000 feet (3,600 m). Even in the harsh climates of northern latitudes, a few species may be found. The wood frog, for instance, makes a home as far north as the arctic circle in Alaska's Brooks Range.

In the process of adapting to a variety of habitats around the world, frogs have also developed some extreme characteristics. The South American horned frog, for example, has large, well-developed fangs which it uses to attack and eat snakes, birds, and small mammals. Also in South America, dozens of species of dart poison frogs have developed toxic skin secretions so poisonous that, as their name suggests, the substance is used by human hunters on arrows and darts. These kinds of highly-toxic frogs typically have bright body colors, a natural method of warning predators to find something else to eat. In Madagascar, the tomato frog is also known for its color — a bright, shiny red.

In Malaysia, the Asiatic horned frog has prominent bony projections over its nose and eyes. In Central America, the spatulate-

SCIENTIFIC CLASSIFICATION

KINGDOM	• Animals
PHYLUM	• Chordata (vertebrates)
CLASS	• Amphibia (amphibians)
ORDER	• Anura (frogs and toads)
FAMILY	• Ranidae (frogs)
GENUS	• Rana (true frogs)
SPECIES	• Rana catesbeiana (bullfrog)

WORLD FROGS

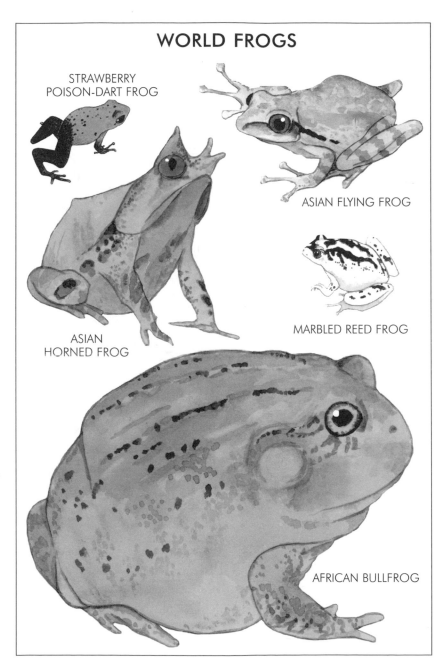

STRAWBERRY
POISON-DART FROG

ASIAN FLYING FROG

ASIAN
HORNED FROG

MARBLED REED FROG

AFRICAN BULLFROG

89

nosed treefrog has an elongated nose that makes it look almost like a miniature alligator. Another Asian frog with a strange body is the Asiatic gliding frog, capable of soaring for distances of up to fifty feet using its large, webbed feet to plane through the air.

The water-holding frogs in the Outback of Australia absorb water into their skin during infrequent rains. Burrowing into the ground after the rain ends, they can survive on the stored water for three or more years.

The pygmy marsupial frog lives in South America and differs from most other frogs in the way it reproduces. A special pouch on the back of females holds fertilized eggs; the eggs remain in the pouch for several weeks until they hatch into tadpoles.

The largest frog species anywhere is the goliath bullfrog, also known as the West African bullfrog. Specimens of this animal have reached more than one foot in length. At the other extreme, the smallest frog in the world is probably the rain frog of southeast Asia, which measures less than one-half inch in length.

HYBRIDS

Some species of frogs in North America are known to crossbreed, adding to the confusion as to which species is which. Hybrid pairs include:

leopard frogs and pickerel frogs
southern chorus frogs and western chorus frogs
green frogs and northern leopard frogs
Unconfirmed: mink frog and green frog

TOADS

"The instrument with which Mr. Tree-Toad catches insect food is his tongue, and it is an extraordinary one of its kind." — Ernest Ingersoll (*The Wit of the Wild,* 1907)

Toads are very close relatives of frogs. In general, frogs live in or near sources of water and toads do not, but there are frogs that live isolated from water and toads that live in watery environments. The scientific classification of animals is also continually changing, shifting some frogs into toad categories and vice versa. For the purposes of this book, only frogs are featured, even though toads are such close relatives. In North America, there are five toad families according to the most recent classification scheme.

TRUE TOADS

American toad (*Bufo americanus*)
Arizona toad (*Bufo microscaphus*)
arroyo toad (*Bufo californicus*)
black toad (*Bufo exsul*)
Canadian toad (*Bufo hemiophrys*)
cane toad (*Bufo marinus*)
Colorado River toad (*Bufo alvarius*)
Fowler's toad (*Bufo fowleri*)
great plains toad (*Bufo cognatus*)
green toad (*Bufo debilis*)
Gulf Coast toad (*Bufo valliceps*)
Houston toad (*Bufo houstonensis*)

oak toad (*Bufo quercicus*)
red-spotted toad (*Bufo punctatus*)
Sonoran green toad
   (*Bufo retiformis*)
southern toad (*Bufo terrestris*)
Texas toad (*Bufo speciosus*)
western toad (*Bufo boreas*)
Woodhouse's toad
   (*Bufo woodhousii*)
Wyoming toad (*Bufo baxteri*)
Yosemite toad (*Bufo canorus*)

NARROWMOUTH TOADS

eastern narrowmouth toad (*Gastrophryne carolinensis*)
great plains narrowmouth toad (*Gastrophryne olivacea*)

FROGS VS. TOADS

Most of the characteristics that make frogs and toads different vary enough that they are useful only as general guidelines in separating the two groups.

BODIES Frogs usually have narrower bodies; toads usually have wider, squatter bodies.

LEGS Frogs have longer, more powerful rear legs.

SKIN Frogs typically have moist or slimy skin that may be smooth, rough, or warty; toad skin is dry and warty.

EGGS Most frogs lay eggs in gelatinous masses; toads lay eggs in long strings.

OTHER Frogs may have a dorsolateral fold that runs from the back of the eardrum all or part of the way to their rear; toads have an L-shaped cranial crest between and behind their eyes. Toads also have a raised parotid gland behind the eye and lack teeth.

HABITATS Most frogs live near bodies of water and spend part of their time in the water; toads do not need to live near water, using water only to breed and lay eggs.

BURROWING TOADS
Mexican burrowing toad (*Rhinophrynus dorsalis*)

SOUTHERN SPADEFOOT TOADS
Couch's spadefoot toad (*Scaphiopus couchii*)
eastern spadefoot toad (*Scaphiopus holbrookii*)
Hurter's spadefoot toad (*Scaphiopus hurterii*)

WESTERN SPADEFOOT TOADS
great basin spadefoot toad (*Spea intermontana*)
New Mexico spadefoot toad (*Spea multiplicata*)
plains spadefoot toad (*Spea bombifrons*)
western spadefoot toad (*Spea hammondii*)

COMMON NORTH AMERICAN TOADS

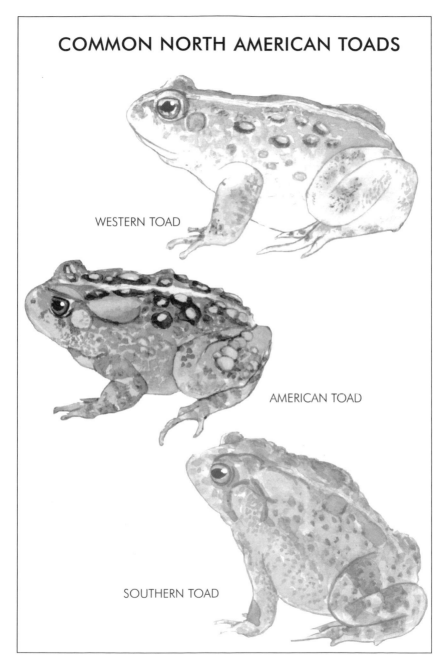

WESTERN TOAD

AMERICAN TOAD

SOUTHERN TOAD

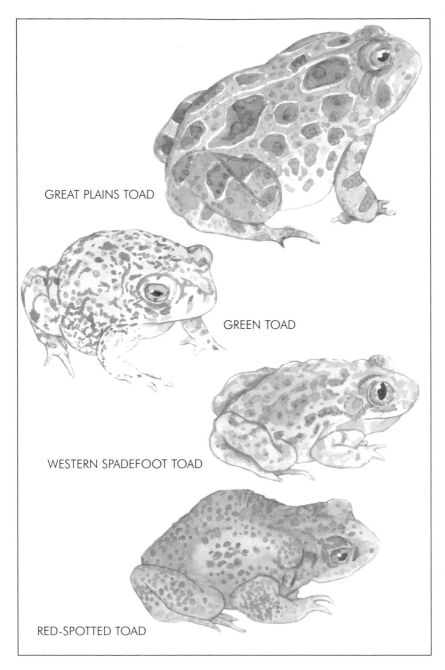

GREAT PLAINS TOAD

GREEN TOAD

WESTERN SPADEFOOT TOAD

RED-SPOTTED TOAD

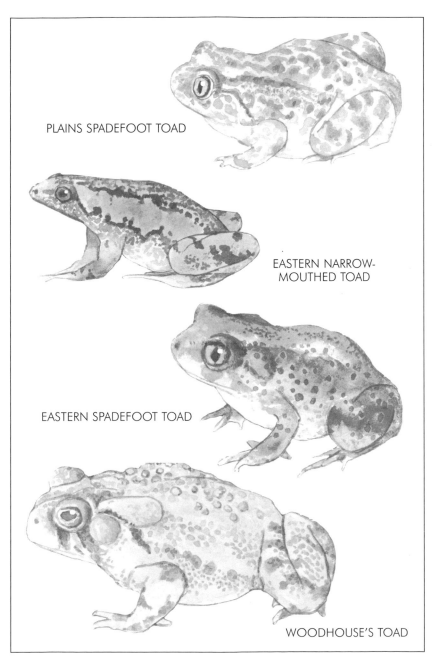

PLAINS SPADEFOOT TOAD

EASTERN NARROW-
MOUTHED TOAD

EASTERN SPADEFOOT TOAD

WOODHOUSE'S TOAD

FROG ANATOMY

"I hold it to be impossible for any one to make a correct description of an animal which has the power of changing its color at will, unless he has it alive ..."

— John Le Conte
(*Descriptive Catalogue of the Ranina of the United States,* 1856)

More people may have an intimate familiarity with the structure of frogs than any other animal. This is mostly the result of decades of high school and college biology classes, where millions of frogs have been dissected in the process of illustrating how vertebrates differ from other kinds of animals.

Frogs have many characteristics that link them to other animals, as well as features that are well-suited to their behavior and choice of habitat. Like other amphibians, they are suited for life both on land and in the water. They have a body shape and limb structure that facilitates swimming; protective coloration that hides them while out of the water; strong legs to jump away from danger; the capability of communication through voice; discriminating hearing to recognize mates and rivals; and eyesight that is adapted to spotting the movement of prey. Treefrogs also have specialized toes that give them a secure grip in the vertical environment in which they live. For all frogs, a uniquely-developed tongue provides a swift and accurate method of capturing their food source.

Although aspects of their digestive systems and circulation are different from other animals, it is their skin that marks them truly distinct from other lifeforms. This flexible, permeable membrane can transmit both gases and fluids, adding a practical method of controlling their internal temperature without the sophisticated metabolisms of higher animal forms. Even though they may be "cold-blooded," they have proven remarkably adaptable to a wide range of temperatures, elevations, and habitats.

SKIN

The outer covering of frogs provides them with an ideal material to escape detection from predators. In fact, the skin of most amphibians has evolved to this degree, permitting these animals to efficiently blend in with their surroundings. The camouflage effect is created by three elements: surface texture, color, and pattern.

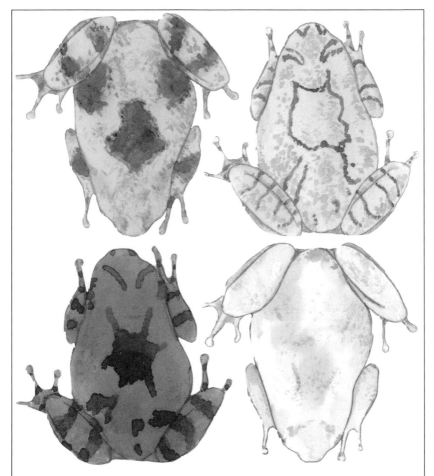

A single species of frog can have a wide variety of colors and patterns and a single frog can also change its own colors and patterns.

FROG SKELETON

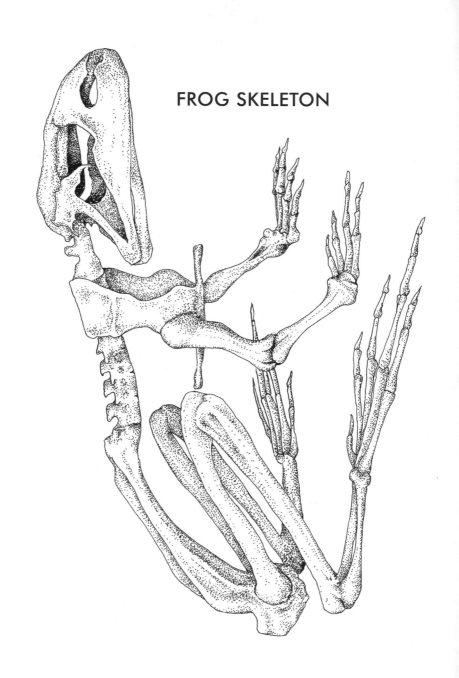

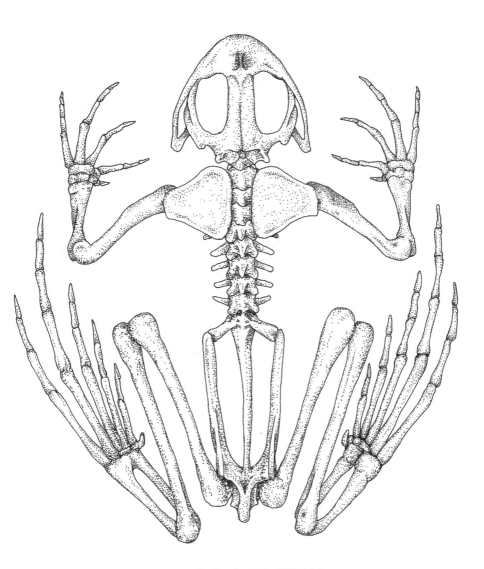

FROG SKELETON

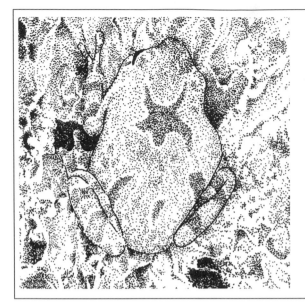

The color and pattern of a frog's skin provides effective camouflage for a variety of conditions. This gray treefrog is ideally suited to blend in with the bark of a tree.

The texture of frog skin ranges from smooth to extremely rough. It can be an uneven surface of ridges, bumps, and warts that mimics the mottled effect of the terrain or plants of the surrounding terrain. Among some species, this surface texture may vary according to a range of habitats, with some frogs in a species having smoother or rougher skin than others. Some biologists have classified frog species in the past by this characteristic, because it corresponds with regional populations and was thought to identify different species. But recent analysis shows that, just like in humans, variations in outward appearance do not necessarily distinguish one type of frog from another.

Color and pattern in the skin surface of frogs is one of the most visible characteristics of the nature of their camouflage. With few exceptions, frogs in North America feature colors that are common in natural materials, including plants, tree bark, soil, and rocks. Browns and greens predominate.

In addition to a basic underlying color, stripes, spots, and irregular markings create visual patterns that add to the camouflage effect. Most species in North America exhibit some degree of variation in these colors and patterns, with a few species characterized by such a wide range of variation that the frogs in question can rarely be accurately identified just from their color and pattern alone.

Among all the North American frogs, treefrogs are noted for the most extreme camouflage. Some species of these small amphibians are so camouflaged, in fact, that they can rarely be spotted unless they are in the act of vocalizing or moving.

Frogs have the ability to change the color of their skin, improving its ability to blend in with its surroundings, but in North American species, few frogs actively use this function. A hormone secreted by the pituitary gland reacts to changes in light and texture around the animal's body, stimulating the body to increase or decrease the production of melanin — a dark pigment — in various locations. The color change actually comes from two different processes, one that is quick — requiring only a few seconds and lasting from a few minutes to a few hours — and one that is slow — developing gradually over a period of hours and lasting from days to months.

Color change is also a characteristic of the breeding season, at least for the males of some species. Their vocal sacs may intensify in color or change color completely, becoming brighter and, like the mating look for many other types of animals, more attractive to females, as well as a warning sign to other males.

Albino frogs will occasionally appear among most species. These pale animals lack pigment in their skin but may not be completely colorless. Sometimes, the albino condition only affects the pigment, or melanin, in parts of the frog's color pattern. Albino frogs may have pink, white, or a similar shade of color. The eyes of albinos are typically red or pink.

Frog bodies are about 70 to 80 percent water, but they can afford to lose little of this. Skin is their primary means of supplying this water and maintaining it. Unlike the skin of most other animals, it is a permeable organ, open to the moisture of the surrounding atmosphere. On dry land, frogs will actually lose moisture from their bodies through evaporation unless the air is unusually humid. Different species of frogs lose or gain water through their skin at different rates and for some species, when fully submerged in water, the rate of absorption slows, a useful feature that keeps the frog's body from becoming waterlogged. But when excess water is being absorbed, it is typically processed rapidly into urine and passed out again.

Unlike other animals, almost all of the water that frogs add to their bodies does not come from drinking it through their mouths. Water gain comes from absorption through the skin, from the food they eat, and in extreme cases, by diverting it from their bladders or other internal stores.

The moisture that leaves a frog's body through the skin is concentrated in special skin glands. Under normal conditions, a typical frog near a watery habitat will feel wet or slippery when touched, the result of the release of this moisture from their body.

One of the major health threats to frogs is an excess loss of water. If they lose too much, they may become paralyzed or die. To reduce water loss, frogs change their behavior to conserve what water they already have. During dry conditions — during the day or during a prolonged seasonal period — they will move into the shade, burrow into the ground, or seek shelter in caves or other protected openings. A few species in North America also can resort to more drastic methods, producing a sort of cocoon made of discarded layers of skin and mucous. Encased in this kind of self-made shelter, the frogs have a dramatically slowed metabolism and can withstand months of arid conditions. A different kind of protective shield is produced by a few species of North American treefrogs, including the green treefrog and the spring peeper. In their lofty habitats, they are typically more exposed to the drying conditions of the sun and wind, and have developed a method to slow down the natural evaporation of moisture through their skin. However, scientists have not yet figured out how this method works.

Along with the glands that hold water, there are specialized glands in the skin of frogs that produce sticky, poisonous compounds as a means of self protection. At one extreme, these poisons are toxic enough to kill humans, but for most frogs, including those found in North America, the toxicity is much less powerful, able to irritate but not to kill. When grabbed or threatened by a predator, secretions from a frog's poison glands are triggered, sometimes causing the predator to drop or spit out the offending animal.

Frog skin is not a permanent part of their bodies. It is constantly growing and the outer layer molts or sheds periodically. Many species of frogs dispose of the shedding skin by eating it. The skin molts often in some species, every few days or few weeks. In some cases, the molting begins with the old skin separating and splitting along the center of the back. Frogs who lose their skins in this manner may actively work to remove it, pulling their front and hind legs out of the old skin.

EYES

Frogs, characteristic of all amphibians, lead a double life: part on land and part in the water. Their eyes reflect this lifestyle with a design that allows them to see underwater as well as in the air. This is not a simple feature, as light travels differently through water than through air. One of the ways their eyes have adapted to this dual role is in the method of focus. With mammals (as well as birds and reptiles), eyes change focus by changing shape, an action performed by the muscles that surround these organs. Amphibians, on the other hand, cannot change the shape of their eyes in order to change the focus; the function is performed by a special set of muscles that move only the lens.

The frog eye has many characteristics that are shared with the eyes of other animals, including mammals. A lens, retina, and other components accept and process light in a similar fashion to those in other animals, with some exceptions. Rods and cones, the structures which react to light, are distributed evenly throughout the frog's eye and there is no fovea, a centralized area without rods that provides enhanced sensitivity in mammals.

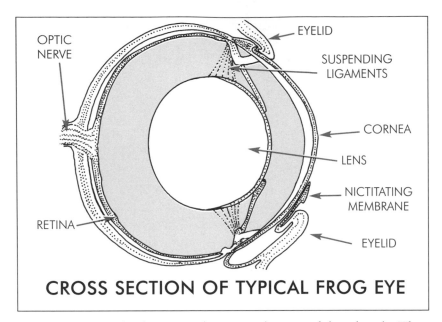

OPTIC NERVE	EYELID
	SUSPENDING LIGAMENTS
	CORNEA
	LENS
	NICTITATING MEMBRANE
RETINA	EYELID

CROSS SECTION OF TYPICAL FROG EYE

Frog eyes are also large in relation to the size of their heads. They use sight more than any other sense to spot and capture food, so their eyes are therefore their most important sense.

Iris color varies in frogs. Some kinds of frogs have black irises, while others may be brown or green, blending in with their skin color. Also part of their overall camouflage, some frogs have a dark streak running horizontally across their eyes, continuing a color stripe that runs along the sides of their heads and bodies. The irises of a few kinds of treefrogs may have gold flecks, and some may be more brightly colored, such as red or orange.

Due to the unique characteristics of the retinas in frog eyes, they seem to have stronger response to blue light than to light of other wavelengths. In some laboratory experiments, frogs that were forced to jump when lights of different colors were provided, most often jumped in the direction of blue lights. In general, frogs that are typically active during the day seem to have a better system of recognizing color than do frogs that are active at night. One experiment using a frog native to Europe indicates that at least this one species

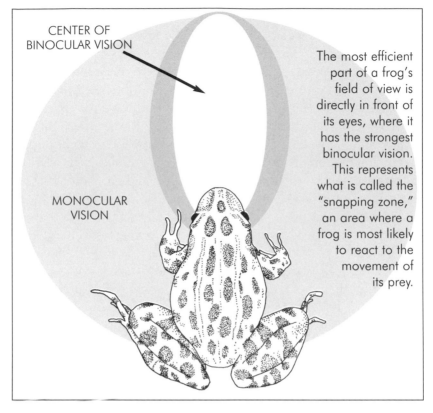

CENTER OF
BINOCULAR VISION

MONOCULAR
VISION

The most efficient part of a frog's field of view is directly in front of its eyes, where it has the strongest binocular vision. This represents what is called the "snapping zone," an area where a frog is most likely to react to the movement of its prey.

of frog, if not others, have a range of color vision that is almost the same as that in humans, being able to differentiate between eight basic colors, and not confusing them with shades of gray.

The most unique fact about the eyes of frogs, however, lies in their ability to cover a wide field of view. In fact, frogs have the widest field of view of all vertebrates, almost 360 degrees in some species. This range comes primarily from how the eyes are situated, extending out and away from the head and therefore open to an unblocked range of sight. The field of view is also expanded because the eyes are wide apart, providing a broad sweep around the frog's head.

Along with this expanse of sight, frogs have an extended form of binocular vision, extending to both sides and above and below their central sightline. Studies have shown the area of binocular vision begins as low as 55 degrees below the central axis of the eyes and ends 170 degrees above. Although this feature of eyesight is a primary factor in hunting success for mammals and some other types of animals — owls for example — frogs do not have to rely on this "stereoscopic" characteristic as a primary tool. Rather, the wide field of view and binocular vision serve more to provide visual input for the motion of their prey than the identification of its exact location. In tests using frogs with only one eye exposed, their ability to track and catch prey was not much different than when using both eyes.

Frog eyes are adapted more for seeing at a slight distance than up close. This feature improves their ability to spot movement that may indicate a meal or danger. The distance is not great, however, no more than thirty to fifty feet. At extremely short distances, a few inches from their head, they may not see much of anything.

In laboratory tests, frog eyes have proven most capable of performing a single type of function. This is the identification of small, moving dark objects. Large objects are less noticeable to them, as are nonmoving objects. Not surprisingly, most of what they depend on for food comes in the form of insects, usually small, moving dark objects.

Because frogs are mobile and actively move through an environment filled with potentially harmful objects, their eyes must have some form of protection. This is provided by three sets of eyelids. Upper eyelids work in tandem with the eyes themselves, closing or opening when the eye itself moves in and out. Lower eyelids can be controlled independently of the movement of the eyes, opening and closing when necessary. A third protective feature is a nictitating membrane, a thin layer of tissue hidden behind the lower eyelids. Depending on the species of frog, it varies from completely transparent to translucent. This membrane closes over the eye whenever the frog is in or under the water. It can also flick across the eyes when the frog is out of the water, performing a useful function by cleansing and moistening the surface of the eye.

An even more remarkable trait is associated with the eyes of frogs: If part of either eye is damaged or destroyed, it will regenerate itself.

At the back of their eyes, most frog species have a thin layer of tissue known as the tapetum lucidium. At night, this layer reflects light and may help with vision. It also helps humans spot frogs in the dark, as it reflects the light from flashlights or floodlights. Toads lack this feature.

EARS

Frogs have reasonably good hearing, a function that helps them identify and locate potential mates, other frogs that may be intruding in their territory, and potential threats from predators or unknown sources. Some frogs are also able to hear and react to the sound of rain and other weather phenomena, a practical function that can trigger life-sustaining action in parts of the continent where rainfall is rare.

The external, visible part of a frog ear is actually an eardrum, or tympanum. Located just behind and below the eyes on the sides of the head, these structures are round or almost round and have a simple, flat surface. Some species have unique markings on the eardrum, while others have noticeable differences in the diameter which may mark the difference between males and females, with males usually having the larger set. Species such as the bullfrog feature very visible eardrums; those in many treefrogs are very difficult to see as they are small and have colors and patterns that blend in with the rest of the head and body.

The inner ear has two separate sound-receiving areas, both based on specialized sensory hairs. Each of these two areas is "tuned" to different frequency ranges, one triggered by higher frequencies and the other by low ranges. For frogs, the total range of hearing is roughly 400 to 4000 Hz.

Some frogs do not receive and process all sound signals the same way. They listen either for higher frequencies that include the vocalizations of other frogs or for low frequencies that include the sounds of approaching predators. In a few species, the bullfrog, for

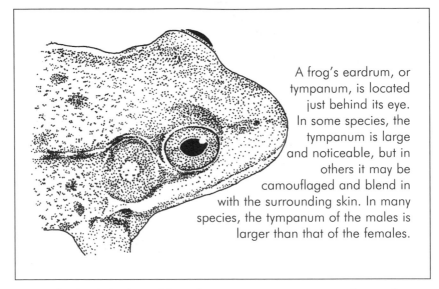

A frog's eardrum, or tympanum, is located just behind its eye. In some species, the tympanum is large and noticeable, but in others it may be camouflaged and blend in with the surrounding skin. In many species, the tympanum of the males is larger than that of the females.

example, both high and low frequencies are monitored together in order to identify calls from other frogs of the same species.

The choice of which sound type to focus on is made in the inner ear, where a unique structure can be manipulated. In one position, the ear system is physically linked to the frog's skeleton in the vicinity of its shoulder, near where the inner ear structure is located. In this position, vibrations are picked up from the ground through the bones in the feet and shoulder and sent as auditory vibrations to the brain. When this low-frequency system is unlinked, an action controlled by special muscles in the middle ear, a frog may gain a useful advantage in some situations. When listening for mating calls, for example, the absence of the low-frequency link helps the frog to filter out confusing and unwanted noises that might hinder its efforts to breed.

TONGUE

The main tool used by the frog to capture food is its tongue. Sticky, fleshy, and flexible, the tongue is attached to the front of the mouth in the lower jaw. Tongue size and length varies from species to species, but typically for all frogs, it is larger and fleshier away from the base and can extend up to, or more than, the length of the body. The tongue is, in effect, "hinged" at the front and the tip lies toward the back of the mouth when not in use. In action, the tip is flipped out from the back of the mouth by the contraction of a highly complex set of muscles attached to the floor of the mouth. As the tip flips, it turns 180 degrees and strikes forward and out of the mouth. This action temporarily turns the soft fleshy tongue into a stiff projectile. As it strikes its target, a sticky coating glues the prey onto the tongue. This coating is a secretion produced by special glands in the base of the tongue and the roof of the mouth.

When the tongue retracts, carrying a smaller animal destined to be food for the frog, the animal is swallowed whole. For prey too large to swallow easily, frogs may struggle to force the food into their mouths, sometimes using one or both front legs to cram it in. Frogs also have another unique feeding characteristic. As they swallow, they close and retract their eyes. Due to the structure of frog skulls, the lower part of their eyes protrude into their mouths. By retracting their eyes, the movement helps push food down their throats.

Frogs have the ability to smell and taste, but these take a secondary position to the value of vision in finding and identifying

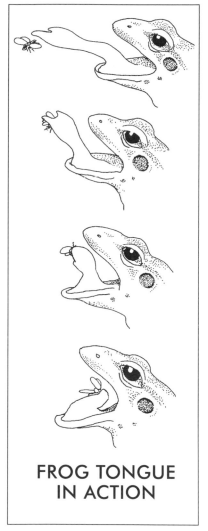

FROG TONGUE IN ACTION

food. Frogs may also use some odor signals to help in orientation and migration, and for some species, as an added incentive during the mating season. In the water, odor may help indicate the presence of predators.

Most frogs do not seem to pay much attention to the taste of the food they eat, voraciously swallowing about anything that comes within range. But a sense of taste is present and may help in identifying and rejecting some potentially toxic food sources, including other frogs with toxic secretions.

FEET AND LEGS

The leg bones of the frog have developed unique characteristics that are involved with jumping and hopping. More so than in most animals, the rear legs of frogs are unusually long, creating efficient levers for jumping. The bones of the forearm, the radius and ulna, are fused, as are the tibia and fibula, the bones of their lower rear legs. Referred to as the radioulna and the tibiofibula, respectively, these adaptations produce a stronger structure that improves their jumping effectiveness. Bones in the ankles of their rear legs are also longer than similar bones in other animals, adding to the power and leverage needed for leaping.

The frog uses its legs for more than locomotion. Specialized toes

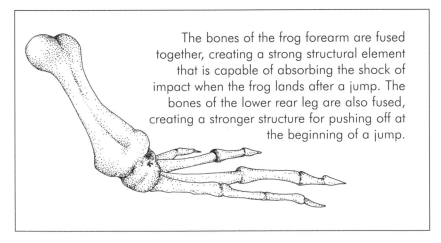

The bones of the frog forearm are fused together, creating a strong structural element that is capable of absorbing the shock of impact when the frog lands after a jump. The bones of the lower rear leg are also fused, creating a stronger structure for pushing off at the beginning of a jump.

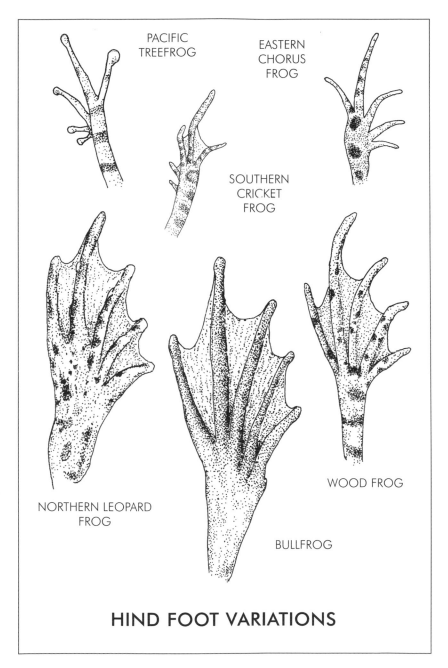

PACIFIC
TREEFROG

EASTERN
CHORUS
FROG

SOUTHERN
CRICKET
FROG

NORTHERN LEOPARD
FROG

WOOD FROG

BULLFROG

HIND FOOT VARIATIONS

give unique advantages in several habitats, including underwater and high in the treetops. Frogs that spend much of their life in the water have extensive webbing between their rear toes, a feature that improves power when swimming. This webbing is not found on the front toes of most species. Webbing varies from species to species, on some frogs extending from the base of the toes to the tips; on other species, the webbing may end at the first or second toe joint and there may be uneven webbing lengths between different sets of toes.

On their front legs, both frogs and toads have four fingers and on their rear legs, they have five. North American frogs do not have claws or nails at the tips of their front or rear feet. The only exception is the aptly-named African clawed frog, but this animal is not native to the continent.

Treefrogs and tropical frogs have specially adapted toes that help them move around on terrestrial surfaces. At the end of their toes are enlarged toepads, each consisting of a series of tile-like extensions separated by deep grooves. These surfaces provide the clinging power that keeps them securely fastened to nonhorizontal surfaces. Adhesion comes from capillary action produced by the moisture naturally present on the surfaces of their habitat, but when necessary, a thin, sticky mucous can be produced by special toe glands to coat the toepads. The surface of these toepads is sticky enough to allow them to climb up even smooth and slippery vertical surfaces, such as glass.

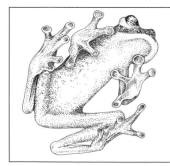

The toe pads of climbing frogs, such as this treefrog, are specially adapted to providing a secure, clinging connection to surfaces such as leaves and bark. On some smooth surfaces, including glass, a thin mucous is secreted from the toepads to improve the adhesion.

REPRODUCTION

"An immense crop of batrachians have come to life more suddenly than mushrooms. Where have all these frogs been during the long dry season?"

— John Muir (journal entry, January 31, 1869)

Most frogs have seasonal breeding cycles or breed when wet conditions trigger this response. In other parts of the world, primarily in humid tropical environments, some frog species may breed throughout the year. But for breeding to happen at all for frogs and other amphibians, much less to be successful and produce babies that are likely to survive, breeding has to be timed to take advantage of the presence of water, a necessary part of the frog reproductive cycle. In most of North America, temperature also plays a major role, triggering breeding in some species and limiting breeding to times when developing frogs will find abundant sources of food.

Frogs have evolved to time their breeding in sync with appropriate seasons. For many species, this means an internal sense that may rely on the changing length of day — the number of hours of daylight — the height of the sun in the sky, or a developing pattern of temperature change over a period of days or weeks. And because frog species across the continent are exposed to a wide range of seasonal variations in weather, different frogs have different responses to the local seasonal changes.

Some frog species have a single breeding season during a year, others have more than one. Frogs that often have two clutches in a year include gray treefrogs, western chorus frogs, green frogs, and bullfrogs. Florida leopard frogs typically have three clutches a year. Females in some species have single clutches when they first begin reproducing, and in later years, have more than one brood. Female bullfrogs follow this pattern.

In other species, there may be varied habits among a population,

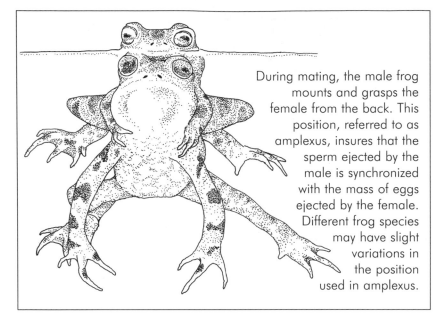

During mating, the male frog mounts and grasps the female from the back. This position, referred to as amplexus, insures that the sperm ejected by the male is synchronized with the mass of eggs ejected by the female. Different frog species may have slight variations in the position used in amplexus.

with some individuals breeding twice or three times and others only once. Species where this variation is seen include green treefrogs, barking treefrogs, and Pacific treefrogs. A few species are at the other extreme, sometimes skipping a year between reproduction cycles. The Oregon spotted frog is one of these, breeding only every second or third year. The tailed frog is also an intermittent breeder, laying eggs every other year.

Unusually long, warm, or wet springs or summers may cause some species to breed more than once. In the dry regions of the southwest, however, a few frog species only breed when local conditions are ripe, meaning warm and wet. These frogs may sometimes miss a year if rainfall is missing or low.

Not all frogs begin reproducing at the same age. Some species of tropical frogs in South America can begin breeding when they are only six to nine months old, but in North America, most frogs do not begin breeding until they are one year old or older. Female Oregon spotted frogs take from five to six years before breeding; males mature at four years. Female bullfrogs usually don't begin breeding until they are three years old and males when they are two to three years old.

At some higher elevations and in more northerly locations, frogs don't begin reproducing until they are between two and four years old. Even among frogs of the same species, those that live at higher elevations or farther north breed later in life than their relatives. In Michigan, for example, populations of the northern leopard frog may take up to two years longer to begin breeding in the northern part of the state than populations in the southern region. In Maryland, the same kind of age gap exists for wood frogs living in the highlands compared to those located in the lowlands.

In a local population of frogs, the approach of appropriate breeding weather may only be the first stage in preparation for reproduction. Many frog species rely on mass matings to insure the survival of offspring; large groups of eggs and tadpoles are more likely to survive predation than individual ones. If this kind of mating is to occur, all of the frogs in the local population must synchronize their breeding. Temperature is the most important factor in this synchronization, triggering this group mating when the internal temperature of the cold-blooded frog reaches a critical point. A rainstorm that occurs just at the right time can result in widespread mating action.

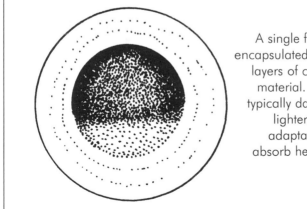

A single frog egg may be encapsulated in one or more layers of clear, gelatin-like material. The egg itself is typically darker on top and lighter underneath, an adaptation that helps it absorb heat from the sun.

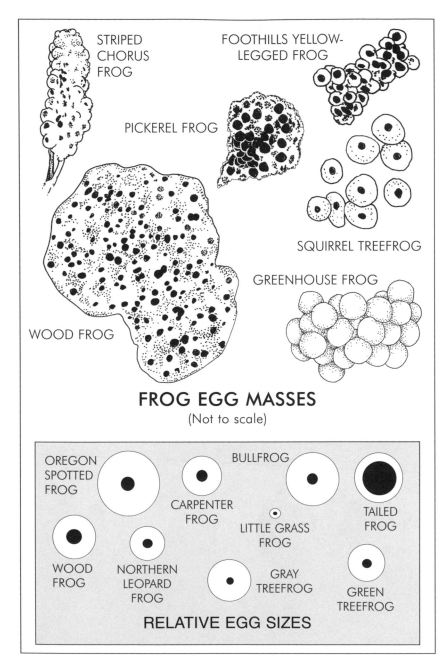

STRIPED CHORUS FROG

FOOTHILLS YELLOW-LEGGED FROG

PICKEREL FROG

SQUIRREL TREEFROG

GREENHOUSE FROG

WOOD FROG

FROG EGG MASSES
(Not to scale)

OREGON SPOTTED FROG

BULLFROG

CARPENTER FROG

LITTLE GRASS FROG

TAILED FROG

WOOD FROG

NORTHERN LEOPARD FROG

GRAY TREEFROG

GREEN TREEFROG

RELATIVE EGG SIZES

In some frog species, chorus calling may also be involved in organizing the breeding activity of a local population. The calls made by males to establish and maintain territory and summon females can also serve as a physiological signal that turns on the reproductive urges in all of the other male frogs in the chorus at the same time. Some biologists have also found that the male chorus, changing tune during the breeding season, may trigger all of the females in the area to begin ovulating at the same time.

During their reproductive season, males of some frog species develop special color changes. In North America, most of these examples are limited to the vocal sacs, which may take on a brighter hue of the existing color or change color completely.

As a general rule, frog species that use temporary bodies of water for reproduction mate in short, synchronized actions that may involve hundreds or thousands of individual frogs and last only for a night or two. Species that rely on permanent bodies of water may have mating behavior that is unsynchronized and can last over a period of weeks or months. Mass matings can be a frenzied, unor-

FROG EGGS

TYPE OF FROG	ESTIMATED NUMBER OF EGGS	DESCRIPTION OF EGG MASS
Blanchard's cricket frog	200–400	singles, small clusters
bullfrog	5,000–20,000	single floating cluster
gray treefrog	1,000–2,000	small clusters
green frog	1,000–5,000	single floating cluster
mink frog	500–4,000	globular clusters
northern cricket frog	200–400	singles, small clusters
northern leopard frog	300–6,000	globular cluster
pickerel frog	800–3,000	globular cluster
spring peeper	750–1,300	singles, small clusters
striped chorus frog	500–1,500	loose clusters
wood frog	500–3,000	several clusters

ganized activity, with little discrimination by males or females for mating partners. The object here is to mate quickly to give the next generation the best chance at survival. In these situations, males may fight for access to females, a common occurrence when there are more males than females present.

Those frogs that follow a prolonged breeding period rely on more picky encounters in order for mating to occur. In these cases, the males' territories are usually well-established and heeded during the breeding ritual; these kinds of frogs are less likely to face violent encounters in their quest for mates. For some species, males that have well-defined territories may not be the only ones that are successful in mating. So-called "satellite males" are solitary frogs of the same species that hide within another male's breeding territory but do not participate in the normal calling behavior. If female frogs respond to the defending frog's call, some may encounter and mate with one of the satellite males instead of the one doing the calling. Satellite behavior has been noted with bullfrogs, pacific treefrogs, northern cricket frogs, striped chorus frogs, and spring peepers. (See also "Frog Calls," page 150.)

Frogs are not monogamous, but some will only mate once in a breeding season, with a single male and a single female involved. The males of most species, however, will mate repeatedly as long as females respond to their mating calls.

Frog eggs are fertilized after they leave the female's body. In order for the sperm from the male to have a better chance of fertilizing the eggs in this kind of situation, frogs have developed a mating posture that places the male close to the females as the eggs are ejected. With this behavior, the ejection of both the eggs and the sperm are synchronized. The tailed frog is an exception to this process, with the sperm entering the female before fertilization. Because the tailed frog lives and mates in cold, fast-running mountain streams, this method may have evolved to improve the efficiency of fertilization under harsh conditions.

The behavior that maximizes the connection between sperm and egg is called amplexus, a biological term for the male being on top of the female and grasping her body with his front legs. In many frog species, the males typically have enlarged or altered toes on their front legs in order to improve their grasping power in this position. Most species in North America use a form of amplexus where the male's front legs grasp the female directly behind her front legs. Frog species in other parts of the world may have variations of this posture, with the grasp higher or lower on the female's body. Amplexus not only improves the chances of sperm meeting eggs, the physical act may be a trigger, a signal for the female to begin ejecting the eggs.

Eggs and sperm are ejected simultaneously, with the cloacas of both frogs close together. Some frogs may also use their rear feet during this process to create a protective temporary container for the mass of egg and sperm. Cradling the mass in this manner for a few minutes improves the efficiency of the sperm getting to the eggs.

The egg-laying process may take several minutes or more. When the female has laid all of her eggs, she must create some kind of signal to let the male know that the mating has been accomplished. Some species use release calls that are different from other vocalizations; other species may kick, stretch, or vibrate their bodies to communicate.

Frogs typically lay a lot of eggs. This is a necessary trait in a natural system, where frogs as well as their eggs and tadpoles are close to the bottom of the food chain, preyed upon by a wide variety of hungry predators. As a general rule, the larger the size of the frog species, the more eggs they lay.

Each egg, or ovum, has a transparent layer surrounding it, providing nutrients to the developing egg and protecting it against damage from rough surfaces and some environmental forces, such as ultraviolet radiation. But this layer is not an unyielding barrier; many important things pass through it freely, including oxygen, carbon dioxide, ammonia, and water.

Although this outer coating is an effective defense against most natural forces, various kinds of chemicals, such as those found in industrial pollution, may penetrate it and kill or damage the devel-

FROG DEVELOPMENT COMPARISON

SPECIES	HATCHING TIME FOR EGGS	DEVELOPMENT TIME FOR TADPOLES
tailed frog	30 days	36 months
bird-voiced treefrog	2 days	24 days
green treefrog	2 days	35 days
wood frog	20 days	67 days
bullfrog	20 days	12 months
mink frog	4 days	12 months
Oregon spotted frog	14 days	85 days
red-legged frog	42 days	100 days
crawfish frog	11 days	150 days
Strecker's chorus frog	5 days	60 days
mountain chorus frog	5 days	55 days
spring peeper	6 days	45 days
green treefrog	2 days	35 days

NOTE: These times are averages based on published reports.

oping embryo. In some kinds of frogs — red-legged frogs, wood frogs, and possibly other species — biologists have also found another intruder. Certain kinds of unicellular algae grow within the gelatinous capsule, arriving shortly after the eggs are laid. There may or may not be a beneficial relationship between this algae and the developing eggs; scientists have yet to reach a conclusion.

Egg size varies among different species of frogs. In general, the larger the egg, the larger the frog that laid it. Another general relationship has been found between elevation and egg size, with larger eggs laid at higher elevations. The same change seems to apply with latitude, with egg size increasing the farther north the habitat of the frog in question. The effects produced by elevation and latitude may have something to do with temperature because water is generally colder at higher elevations and in locations farther north, but this theory has yet to be proven.

Another relationship that is also affected by the size of the eggs is the time it takes for an egg to develop before hatching. In North American species, hatching time varies from only one day to more than a month, with larger eggs generally taking longer. Hatching periods are not fixed, however, and can take less or more time from year to year, or among different populations of the same species. The most important variable affecting this stage of development is temperature, with higher water temperatures resulting in shorter hatching periods.

Older females in some species often lay fewer, larger eggs. Offspring born to these more experienced mothers are therefore more likely to survive and thrive. Local food supplies and seasonal characteristics can also have an effect on how many eggs a frog lays and how large the eggs are.

Size makes a difference to the newly-laid eggs because the larger the egg, the more nutrients it contains. If the developing embryo has more energy available for it to consume before it hatches, it will grow quicker and hatch into a larger and healthier tadpole, improving the animal's chance of survival, and later in its life, improved success at reproducing its own offspring.

Another variation in eggs laid by various species of frogs is the amount of pigment, or melanin, found in the ovum. A general relationship exists between light or uncolored eggs and frogs that lay their eggs in shadowed conditions. Frogs that lay their eggs in exposed sunlight generally have eggs with dark, pigmented centers. This relationship most likely is a practical feature that helps protect the eggs against the damaging effects of ultraviolet radiation, one of the components of sunlight. The dark color is also more effective at absorbing heat from the light, a factor that speeds the development of the embryos. Eggs in masses are even more effective at this type of heat absorption, with groups of eggs storing and sharing the absorbed heat.

Egg masses also provide another important effect: The jelly-like coatings work together to protect the mass against drying out if there is a sudden drop in water level. A study of wood frogs determined that the mass formation helped some eggs survive for up to two weeks after a loss of surrounding water.

Egg masses can be small clusters with a few eggs each or larger clusters of hundreds. The masses can be loose and ragged in shape or tight and compact; some frogs produce globular forms and some long, thin strings of eggs. Masses may be laid on the surface of a body of water, just under the surface, near the bottom; they can be floating loose or attached to rocks or leaves and stems of aquatic vegetation. Some frogs, particularly the tropical frogs, lay their eggs in damp conditions, but not in standing water. All of these characteristics vary among the different species and to a trained eye, can even be used to identify the species of frog whose development is underway.

The type of egg mass seems to adapt to the habitat where the parent species breed. In water that is flowing rapidly, for example, eggs that were laid in large masses would produce resistance and tend to be carried away by the current. Habitats with cold water influence large, compact masses, where the combined eggs can absorb and share warmth. Predators are also influential in the types of egg masses, as many predators find them an attractive source of food. Where certain kinds of fish or aquatic insects are part of a long-established ecosystem, the local frog species could not survive unless some of their eggs had a chance to evade these natural hunters. Here, over long periods of time, species success favors egg masses that are hidden or otherwise difficult for predators to find.

The survival of eggs can also be improved by the actions of individual parent frogs. Biologists have noted that several species of North American frogs — bullfrogs and some kinds of treefrogs, for example — are picky about where they lay their eggs. Females favor spots less likely to have egg predators, and mate with those males who select territory based on the same criteria.

TADPOLES

"The child of the rain-makers,
The water frog,
Goes about hurrying his fathers,
*   the rain-makers."*

— Ritual song of the Good Kachina, Zuni Pueblo

All amphibians lead a unique double life. The origin of the word amphibian comes from the Greek words for "double life," referring to the fact that they spend part of their lives in the water and part on land. It could also apply to their unique dual lifeforms, first existing as tadpoles, a stage of life that is physically distinct from the form they later assume as adults. Excluding insects, few other animal forms exhibit such a dramatic change as they grow. To biologists, the tadpole stage of development is referred to as the larval stage of frogs.

Almost all tadpoles hatch from eggs that are laid in clumps or masses of varying sizes. The egg stage of development may last from a few days up to a month or more, depending on the species. The eggs hatch over a period of hours, releasing baby tadpoles. As they hatch, many species retain a group structure, sticking together in loose congregations. This behavior is most common for eggs that are laid in shallow water. Some biologists speculate that these tadpole "schools" are a defensive response to certain predators, such as water beetles. In colonies of tadpoles where some predators such as these are not present, the tadpoles are less likely to clump together. Groups may also have other benefits, including protection against low water temperatures and uncovering more sources of food through feeding agitation off the bottom of a pond.

In a tadpole study of the Cascades frog, tadpoles from the same parents were able to identify each other when placed in mixed groups; their response showed a preference for swimming next to their own brothers and sisters. Further experiments showed that one batch of siblings could also identify tadpoles that were related, even with only one parent in common. When given a preference, these tadpoles preferred swimming with their full siblings first, then half siblings and if given a choice, they chose to be with siblings with a shared mother over a shared father. Tadpoles of wood frogs and red-legged frogs have also demonstrated this kind of recognition capability.

Another grouping preference in some species of tadpoles is based on size. Larger tadpoles of the same species group themselves together, smaller ones do the same. This sorting behavior may help in defense, contributing to the effect of a school in confusing predators.

Frogs lay lots of eggs and therefore, lots of tadpoles are likely to be found together. When more than one frog lays its eggs in the same area, large numbers of tadpoles may find themselves crowded into the same watery environment. But when too many tadpoles are present, the overcrowding can result in stunted growth for some of them. This may come simply because there is less food to be shared, but some tadpoles have also been known to exude natural chemicals that retard growth. More commonly, stress produced by the increased interaction within a dense population does the same thing, which is to slow the rate of growth for the affected animals. When crowding eases, normal growth patterns resume.

Higher water temperatures may cause some species of tadpoles to develop faster. But this doesn't usually lead to larger tadpoles or bigger frogs in the next stage of development. Instead, under ideal conditions, tadpoles just transform quicker and metamorphize at a smaller size.

When a tadpole hatches from the egg, it has gills on the outside of its body through which it absorbs oxygen from the water. Tadpoles that are native to still bodies of water usually have a sticky coating of mucous on the bottom of their heads, a practical feature that sticks them to solid objects until they can begin swimming. From the beginning, all tadpoles have fully functional mouths, necessary to begin eating. Although small, each species of tadpole has

METAMORPHOSIS

- Back legs emerge from fleshy buds, enlarge, and become functional

- Front legs develop inside chambers near the gills, breaking through the skin late in the cycle

- Adult teeth and tongue replace the unique mouthparts of the tadpole form

- The eyes grow larger, their internal structure changes, and eyelids form

- External gills are transformed into internal organs, then absorbed into the body

- Lungs develop independently from the gill system

- The tail is absorbed into the rest of the body, including the degeneration of the tail muscle

- Muscles on the limbs and eyes form

- Skin structure changes into that of adult frog, thickening and developing dermal glands

- The tadpole's sensory system transforms into the nervous system of an adult frog, including internal changes to the brain

- Sexual organs develop

- The kidneys and other parts of the urinary system are transformed

- The intestine of the tadpole, formed to process mostly vegetarian food, changes into a shorter intestine designed to handle the carnivorous diet of adults

- The bony cartilage of the tadpole transforms into adult bone structure

Within days after being laid, a frog egg begins showing visible changes. It can take from a few days to more than a month for a fully-formed tadpole to emerge from the egg, depending on the species.

Most tadpoles turn into frogs quickly, with the transformation happening in a few weeks to a few months, but a few species can take a year or more to make the change.

Even before they have lost all the characteristics of the tadpole lifeform, young froglets may move out of the water and onto land. In some species, the young at this stage may seem to shrink, becoming smaller than their tadpole forms for a short period of time.

TADPOLE METAMORPHOSIS

some distinctive characteristics and herpetologists are able to identify what kind of frog it is by these unique features, including variations in the shape and structure of their mouths.

The tadpoles of different frog species vary in size and shape.
Much of this variation has developed in response to the habitats in
which they live. Tadpoles in still bodies of water, for instance, may
have large fins while tadpoles in streams may have small fins.
Tadpoles raised in fast-running water may also have mouths that are
adapted to fasten to solid objects in order to keep them stationary
in the current.

Tadpoles have a special sensory organ that is only present when
they are in this life stage. This is a lateral line organ that is similar
to that found in fish, a sensitive band of nerves along the side of
their bodies which helps them pick up pressure waves in the water,
improving their ability to detect motion and avoid predators.

Some biologists think of tadpoles as nothing more than specialized eating machines, as this is about the only activity they perform.
Tadpoles feed by filtering food particles through their mouth cavi-
ties and out their gills. Food is constantly collected and filtered, but
they do not have to swim in order to create this filtering action.
This is because the floor of their mouths is flexible, able to create a
pumping action to force water and its contents over their filtering
organs.

Food material that is collected may come from any layer of the
water, from the bottom to the surface. It can include algae, grains of
pollen, protozoans, bacteria, and other particles of organic material.
Larger particles are swallowed directly; minute substances adhere to
sticky threads that coat the filter organs. Tadpoles also have rows of
tiny, tooth-like ridges that they can use for biting, scraping, and
tearing off food from underwater surfaces such as rocks or larger
pieces of debris.

As they eat, tadpoles play a significant part in the ecological
cycles of the bodies of water around them. They reduce the amount
of organic debris that accumulates within the water, turning it into
energy, body mass, and chemical byproducts such as nitrogen. In a

study of one type of frog tadpole, it was found that a single individual "consumed" about 34 fluid ounces (two pints or one liter) of water every day as it fed. With a large number of tadpoles in a single body of water, the total amount of organic material consumed can have a decisive effect on the growth of algae and other plants. Observers have noted that many times, a pond will suddenly "bloom" with algae and other aquatic vegetation after a generation of tadpoles has left the pond to pursue their adult lives.

Tadpoles begin developing into frogs after a few days or weeks. Although the process of transformation into frogs may vary slightly among different species, all tadpoles follow a general order of development. The metamorphosis is triggered and fueled by the secretion of hormones from the thyroid gland. The developmental period is a series of metamorphic stages, beginning with the development of rear legs. As limbs appear, tadpoles may temporarily lose some of their agility in the water, making them more vulnerable to predators. And as they metamorphize, some tadpole species — the wood frog, for example — produce toxins that make them unappetizing or downright poisonous to predators. Before the metamorphosis begins, however, the same tadpoles are nonpoisonous.

Recent studies of tadpole tails reveal another possible defense against predation. Their tails are made of very soft, fragile tissue, which tears easily when grasped by a predator, making them harder to grab and eat. This may be an evolutionary tactic for escape, as tadpoles often survive with lacerated tails.

The tadpole-to-frog alteration is one of the most unique transformations in the animal kingdom. Not only is this process unusual, but it may seem to contradict the usual rule of nature, where animals gain in size as they grow older. For most tadpoles, the opposite is true. When they are in this form, they are often larger than the froglets that they later become. During metamorphosis, some of their body size and mass is absorbed during the energy-intense process. After the young froglet has emerged from its tadpole stage, however, it will begin to grow on its own, and eventually, be larger than the tadpole that it developed from.

TADPOLE VARIETIES

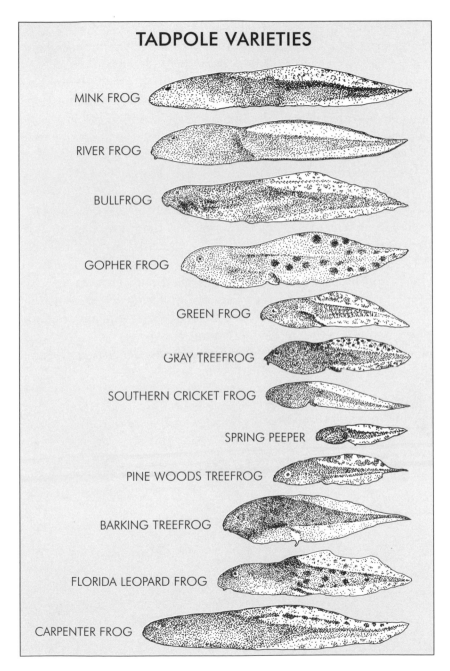

MINK FROG

RIVER FROG

BULLFROG

GOPHER FROG

GREEN FROG

GRAY TREEFROG

SOUTHERN CRICKET FROG

SPRING PEEPER

PINE WOODS TREEFROG

BARKING TREEFROG

FLORIDA LEOPARD FROG

CARPENTER FROG

As tadpoles turn into frogs, they live through a period when some characteristics of their identity from both stages is present at the same time. For example, some tadpoles will develop the front and hind legs of frogs while still consuming a tadpole's diet. At an intermediate stage of metamorphosis, some tadpoles will begin surfacing and gulp air through their developing lungs, but their disintegrating gills will still be functioning. And some baby frogs will emerge from the water to begin their lives on land while they still retain all or part of a tadpole tail.

Most North American frog species have only brief lifespans as tadpoles. After hatching from eggs, the tadpole stage typically lasts from a few weeks to a few months, timed to the warm, damp conditions of the spring and summer seasons. But with the tailed frog, the mink frog, and the bullfrog, tadpole development can last a lot longer. For these species, the tadpole stage usually lasts through the winter, although little growth may occur during the cold period. With the arrival of the next warm season, development resumes. The tailed frog, living in cold, fast-running streams of northern climates, has the longest tadpole stage of all North American frogs, three years.

FROG FOOD

"Lurking in such a place, he becomes an ogre to minute creeping and flying bugs of all sorts, who never notice his gray or green coat until out darts a spoon-like tongue, and they are caught and dragged into his stomach."
— Ernest Ingersoll (*The Wit of the Wild*, 1907)

All of the frogs in North America are carnivores, eating a variety of other animals as their diet. A few frog species in other parts of the world are known to at least occasionally eat fruit or plant material. Tadpoles, on the other hand, are mostly vegetarians, although there are a few exceptions.

Frogs generally have two responses when spotting a potential source of food. One, they will move their body, a little or a lot, to point it more directly at what they expect to catch. Second, they will snap their tongue at the prey, adjusting the direction and distance to match that of the food source. Because most of what they eat are insects, and their surroundings are often damp and attract insects, frogs usually have plenty of food close at hand.

Unlike many other predators, most frogs usually do not stalk their prey. At best, they may make minor adjustments to the position of their bodies if an insect or worm moves away from them, or they may move slightly closer to it to get within range of their tongues. How much or little they pursue food has less to do with their habits and more with how much food is locally available. The green tree-frog, active in habitats where insects are more widely scattered, chases after its food almost 90 percent of the time.

In South America, some frog species have been observed using a wiggling motion of their toes to attract potential prey. This behavior may also be used by some frogs in North America, but if so, it is not widely practiced.

Most of the time, frogs hunt when they are on land or perched on

FOOD SOURCES

aquatic insects	earthworms	salamanders
amphibians	fish	slugs
ants	flies	smaller frogs
baby birds	gnats	snails
bats	grasshoppers	snakes
bees	insect larvae	spiders
beetles	leaf hoppers	springtails
blackflies	leeches	stoneflies
butterflies	mayflies	ticks
caddisflies	mice	turtles
caterpillars	millipedes	wasps
crayfish	mites	water boatmen
crickets	mosquitoes	water striders
damselflies	moths	whirligig beetles
diving beetles	newts	worms
dragonflies	pill bugs	

aquatic vegetation on the surface of ponds or lakes. Sometimes, however, floating or swimming frogs may grab insects that come their way. Bullfrogs have also been observed leaping out of the water to snatch prey out of the air as it flies by.

Frog eyesight is fairly acute, at least from a few feet to a few yards, the distance necessary to identify sources of food. Vision is the primary sense used to spot prey and trigger a hunting response. Most of the time, their vision system requires sensing movement in order to be effective, both in identifying potential food sources and accurately measuring the distance between the food and the frog. In some cases, however, frogs are capable of perceiving objects that they can identify as edible even if no movement is involved.

The feeding response that is triggered in a frog has been studied in several different species. Although the details may differ — varying by species, habitat, size of frog, and other factors — the basics

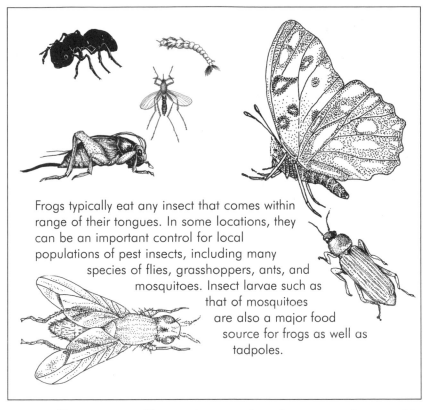

Frogs typically eat any insect that comes within range of their tongues. In some locations, they can be an important control for local populations of pest insects, including many species of flies, grasshoppers, ants, and mosquitoes. Insect larvae such as that of mosquitoes are also a major food source for frogs as well as tadpoles.

are usually consistent. Frogs select prey based on its size (not too big nor too small), its shape (the right ratio of width to height, suggesting a familiar food source), its distance from them, the type of motion (smooth or erratic, for instance), the speed and direction of motion (toward the frog or away from the frog).

All of these factors work together to allow frogs the maximum return on their hunting efforts. They can be indiscriminate eaters, snatching anything that crawls or flies by, but when prey is abundant, they will be more selective. Local food supplies can also influence what a frog is most likely to identify and eat during its adult life. In the first few weeks or months after it has transformed from a tadpole, abundant supplies of specific kinds of insects may "imprint" themselves on a frog's memory. Thereafter, even if given a choice of food, this frog may select and eat more of the food familiar to it from its youth.

The same sophisticated system of prey identification and tracking that allows frogs to eat may also get them in trouble. In a feeding frenzy, frogs may confuse some kinds of inedible moving objects for food. This can include falling leaves, seedpods, or other debris of various types. In extreme cases, frogs may be hurt by ingesting a large amount of such material. Human frog hunters have tradition-ally taken advantage of this tendency by fishing for frogs with noth-ing more than small patches of colored cloth tied to fishing lines or string.

Frogs, unlike toads, have teeth. These are not the same type of structures found in mammals, but hard bony protrusions that are attached loosely at the base. They point toward the back of the frog's mouth, and in most frog species, only occur in the upper jaw. Frog teeth are not permanent, growing in and falling out through-out its adult life. Also unlike mammals, frog teeth are not used for chewing, but serve merely as a handy device for gripping prey and helping move it backward into the throat.

Most of the time, frogs eat while on land or perched out of the water. Bullfrogs, however, are known to carry some prey underwa-ter, where it is ingested.

Tadpoles are "vegetarians," eating mostly algae, diatoms, and decaying plants in their watery environment. In some species, how-ever, such as the bullfrog, tadpoles have been known to feed on decaying animal matter. A few of the North American frog species are also known to be somewhat carnivorous, seeking out a wider variety of animal food. The tadpoles of bullfrogs and wood frogs, for example, frequently eat the eggs and larvae of other frog species and sometimes cannibalize those of their own species. As tadpoles change into froglets, the small frogs begin to eat animals, targeting the smallest forms available to them, mainly mites, midges, spring-tails, and other tiny insects.

When fully grown, North American frogs depend mostly on

insects for food but depending on the physical size of the frog, a variety of other animals may also be part of the diet. Bullfrogs, the largest frog species on the continent, have a well-deserved reputation for eating just about anything that moves and can fit into their mouths. This includes snakes, mink, bats, and rodents. They may eat more exotic fare when the opportunity arises, including small alligators and birds. Many frogs are also major predators of other, smaller frog species. Bullfrogs, for one, are aggressive opportunists and are known to readily snatch and eat any other frog that comes along, providing it is the right size.

About the only thing that frogs are not known to regularly prey upon are toads, their closest relatives. This is because of the toxic secretions that toads exude from their skin, making them unpalatable at best and downright poisonous at worst. But some biologists have found exceptions to this avoidance, citing examples of bullfrogs with partially-digested toad remains in their stomachs.

PREDATORS

"The length of life which these frogs can attain is quite unknown ... it is no exaggeration to say that few, if any, frogs die of old age, since they have so many enemies."

— Hans Gadow (*The Cambridge Natural History, Vol. III, Amphibia and Reptiles*, 1901)

From the time they leave the tadpole stage until they are adults, frogs are a major part of the food chain for many other animals. They are most vulnerable when at their youngest and smallest stage. Fewer than half of all tadpoles escape predators before they meta-morphosize and in some species, only ten percent or less make it past this stage. Froglets of some species have a mortality rate of 95 percent or more, mostly coming from predation, and for most frog species in North America, it is likely that only one or two percent of all eggs produced by females end up as reproducing adults.

Predatory animals begin their consumption of frogs at the egg stage. Like the eggs of many animals, frog eggs are full of nutrition, a necessary feature that provides fuel for the developing embryos. Many animals seek out these eggs, including insects and fish, hunt-ing them from the surrounding watery environment, while birds and mammals seek them from above. Some frog eggs may be distasteful or even toxic, however, being protected by natural chemicals intended to discourage predation.

Once the eggs hatch into tadpoles, predation continues. The tad-poles of most frog species group together in rough schools to provide protection, but they still provide ample food for predators who seek locations where tadpoles are common. A few frogs, such as bull-frogs, may deliberately seek out breeding areas where predators are few, improving the chances of their eggs and tadpoles surviving. Another level of protection for some tadpoles, like with the eggs, comes from natural protective toxins, but none of the species in North America are completely safe with this type of defense.

A wide variety of swimming, climbing, flying, and walking animals prey upon frogs, including other frogs.

The giant water bug and the nymph of the dragonfly are natural predators of frog tadpoles.

FROG PREDATORS

alligators	foxes	raccoons
bats	giant water bugs	shrews
bears	larger frogs	skunks
birds	lizards	snakes
coyotes	mink	spiders
fish	otters	turtles
flying squirrels	possums	wolves

Among the predators who regularly eat frog eggs are aquatic insects, fish, leeches, newts, and turtles.

Tadpoles are preyed upon by a variety of aquatic animals. These include diving beetles, dragonfly nymphs, fish, herons, larger frogs, salamander larvae, spiders, water bugs, water scorpions, and water snakes.

After metamorphosis, frogs rely on natural camouflage to avoid attracting the attention of predators. This camouflage has evolved in response to the characteristics of the habitat that each species favors. By blending into their surroundings, frogs not only decrease the chance of being eaten, they increase their own chances of snatching an unsuspecting meal.

In response to motion toward them that might be considered threatening, frogs rely on both visual signals and vibrations transmitted through the ground. Depending on the circumstances, time of day, the size and shape of the threat, and the species of frog, the response is typical, they attempt to jump out of the way of danger. The direction of the jump, however, is rarely directly away from the oncoming object; most often, the leap is at an angle to the line of motion.

Frogs, being at home in the water and usually staying close to it, also exhibit another unsurprising instinct. When threatened, they will inevitably attempt to leap into the safety of water. Once in the water, frogs typically swim directly away from the shore but then quickly reorient themselves, turning to face the bank and swim back toward their original launching point. The same response has been shown in tadpoles; their initial response is to swim away from a threat and shortly thereafter, to circle back to their original location in the water.

Frogs are extremely vulnerable to predation compared to many other animals, as they have little in the way of built-in protection. Other than avoiding predators in the first place, quick response to danger is their most valuable asset. But even though they are ill-equipped to bite or inflict damage on their attackers, many frogs may be rejected as meals because of the toxic secretions they produce in special glands in the skin. Some fish, snakes, birds, and mammals learn to identify and avoid certain kinds of frogs on sight because of the unpleasant effects of having one in their mouths. Eggs and tadpoles of some species may also be toxic, or at least unpleasant tasting to predators. Some biologists believe that among North American frog species, the ones most likely to have these kind of eggs and tadpoles are those that favor habitats based on permanent bodies of water with resident populations of predatory fish. Frogs that breed in temporary bodies of water, on the other hand, may produce eggs and tadpoles that lack this defense.

Observers have also noted that on occasion, some frogs will fight back if attacked, kicking at their attackers with their back legs. When grabbed, most frogs also emit a particular kind of distress call, a scream that may help to startle some attackers.

Other animals are not the only thing that frogs have to avoid. In parts of the continent, carnivorous plants such as the Venus flytrap can consume unwary treefrogs or other small frogs that move through its habitat.

LOCOMOTION

"To catch two frogs you need two hands."

—traditional Chinese proverb

Frogs and jumping go together like birds and flying. With their unique method of getting about on land, frogs have created a visible symbol of athletic prowess and an identity based on this ability. Not all frogs, however, jump as well as others and some frogs hop more like toads, with short, lumbering movements.

The fact that frogs survive in environments filled with a wide assortment of predators is a powerful recommendation for their jumping abilities. Evolution has favored this kind of locomotion, altering their bodies to make better use of the jumping strength of their hind legs. Bones in the lower legs, both front and rear, have developed a unique structure that enhances this strength, fused together into a single unit working as a shock absorber when landing from a jump (see Anatomy: Legs and Feet).

Some of the ankle bones are also longer than similar bones in other animals and, added to the design of the pelvis and spine, create a framework specialized for jumping. Attached to this frame are powerful and specialized muscles that have developed to do little more than provide short, strong bursts of power.

All of this adaptation adds up to improved jumping performance, but not all frogs are equally good jumpers. The longest jumping frog is the Carpathian frog, native to Europe, which can leap more than nine feet. Large North American frogs such as the bullfrog are able to leap more than five feet and some smaller frogs can jump up to three or four feet, more than ten times their own body length.

To maximize a jump, a frog coordinates its rear legs, both pushing off at the same time. Unlike most jumping activity from other kinds of animals, as frogs jump, the velocity of their movement and the force applied to the ground increases while the legs are still in contact with the ground.

Most of the time, speedy jumps are more critical than distance, as the frog is attempting to get into the safety of water in a single jump rather than merely out-distance a predator. Land-based frogs — tropical frogs and treefrogs, for example — also typically rely on a single jump in reaction to danger, but their leaps end in immobility, with the frog attempting to escape detection with its protective camouflage. Toads characteristically make a series of short hops in response to danger, with many species then resorting to immobility to blend in with the surroundings. The cricket frogs also have a slightly different hopping style, using a series of erratic jumps to reach the safety of water. This jumping pattern, similar to that of crickets, inspired their common name.

The muscle metabolism of frogs is also aimed at short bursts of activity. Muscles are quickly overloaded during escape sequences, leaving a frog temporarily exhausted and unresponsive after only a minute or two of flight. In a sense, frogs might be compared to

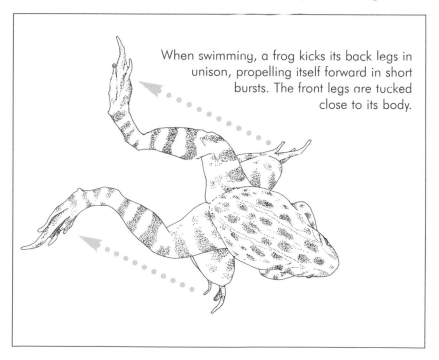

When swimming, a frog kicks its back legs in unison, propelling itself forward in short bursts. The front legs are tucked close to its body.

sprinters, with running muscles developed for maximum speed over a short distance, rather than marathon runners, with highly-developed aerobic conditioning and stamina.

One biological study of leopard frogs shows that even after the major jumping muscles of their rear legs contract to propel the frog forward, a low level of contraction continues, most likely to keep the rear legs straightened, thereby improving the streamlined effect of the body pushing through the air. After launching, a frog lands directly on its front legs. The fused bones of the lower front legs and their relatively short length makes them appropriate shock absorbers.

While swimming or diving, frogs use only their rear legs, tucking their front legs close to their bodies. Limited by the structure of their pelvis, spine, and rear legs, however, their motion in water is

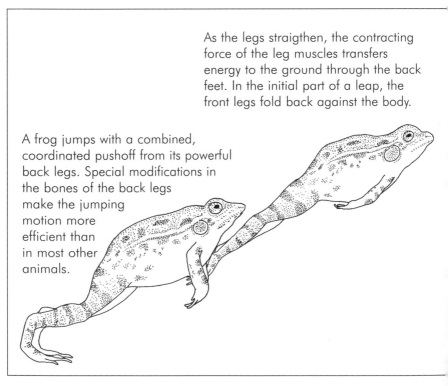

As the legs straigthen, the contracting force of the leg muscles transfers energy to the ground through the back feet. In the initial part of a leap, the front legs fold back against the body.

A frog jumps with a combined, coordinated pushoff from its powerful back legs. Special modifications in the bones of the back legs make the jumping motion more efficient than in most other animals.

very similar to that on land, with the rear legs kicking out and back like the legs of a swimmer doing the breaststroke. If at rest underwater, such as when they are feeding or hiding, the front legs may be used to cling to underwater surfaces.

Climbing frogs are as at home in trees and bushes as other frogs are squatting on floating vegetation. They may hop from perch to perch in their habitats, leaping horizontally or vertically. Slower motions may also be used to creep along rocky, leafy, or woody surfaces. The surface of their toes is what makes this possible (see Anatomy: Legs and Feet), a feature that allows them to cling to a wide variety of surfaces.

Some frogs also dig and burrow to provide a hole for protection from the heat or cold. Either front or back legs may be used in this activity.

As it prepares to land, the frog's front legs extend forward. Special modifications in the bones of the front legs help absorb the force of landing, which happens front feet first.

TEMPERATURE EXTREMES

*"In the autumn, when the nights begin to grow chill,
the leaves fade and fall, and the short life of the insect
world comes to an end, these little frogs grow quiet,
and, descending from their perches to the ground,
seek a snug, warm berth in which to take their
long winter sleep."*

— Ernest Ingersoll (*The Wit of the Wild,* 1907)

Frogs and other amphibians do not have the same control over their body temperature as mammals. To a large extent, they are at the mercy of nature and must use behavior rather than internal regulation to find sources of heat and cold in order to survive. These sources can include water, the air, or the ground. Biologists call this type of metabolism "ectotherm," meaning the control of the body temperature comes from outside the body. In common terminology, they are called "cold-blooded."

Frogs may change their positions during the day or night in order to adjust their temperature. They also must make great accommodations during the colder seasons in order to survive. Internal temperature can be adjusted to a minor degree by altering the rate of breathing. Their unique skin can also retain or evaporate body moisture, aiding in temperature regulation. Some frogs also alter their skin color, not just to improve camouflage, but to absorb or reflect heat from the sun.

Even though they may not thrive when temperatures are low, most frogs have a great tolerance for cold. Some species can withstand internal temperatures as low as 38 degrees F. (3 degrees C.). They can also survive external temperatures of 110 degrees F. (43 degrees C.), but they do not generally have internal temperatures higher than 96 degrees F. (36 degrees C.). The mean internal temperature for frogs is 81 degrees F. (27 degrees C.). As the outside temperature increases or decreases to extremes, however, frogs become sluggish, and will eventually be paralyzed and die if they are exposed for too long a period of time.

Throughout North America, cold is the environmental condition most often encountered by frogs. Seasonal cold is a recurring factor in their life cycles, and for most species, their behavior has developed to allow them to survive during wintry conditions. Some species have ranges that span a wide spectrum of winter conditions, much colder in the north than in the south. These species exhibit a range of tolerance to the cold that corresponds to their local conditions, with frogs in one locality behaving differently than those in another, based on climate.

Experiments with some species have also shown that to some extent, frogs may be able to alter their response to temperature extremes, developing greater tolerance quickly, over a period of only a few days. For a few species — the Rio Grande leopard frog, for example — another biological effect called "temperature hardening" is present. The effect occurs within hours of exposure to extreme temperatures and helps a frog quickly prepare to deal with extremes that may follow. This kind of metabolic feature is different than long term response to temperatures, which is part of the frog's annual life cycle. Experiments have shown that at some times of the year, summer and fall, for example, an amphibian is better able to tolerate high temperature than in the spring.

Winter conditions in most of North America include below-freezing temperatures. Frogs adapt to this condition in a variety of ways, surviving the winter by burrowing into the ground, seeking protection in caves or underground cover, and hiding in muddy banks or the bottoms of streams and ponds. Frogs that are cut off from the air during such periods slow down their breathing rates and metabolism. For many frogs, slow periods of metabolism mean winter-long hibernation. Frog species that hibernate near the surface of the ground where they may be subject to freezing are also thought to have the unique defense of being able to produce antifreeze-like compounds that keep their blood and body tissue from being destroyed by freezing.

Wood frogs are one species known to survive freezing for weeks and months. When frozen, their bodies are rigid, their breathing stops, and their hearts do not beat. As they thaw, they gradually return to a normal state of living.

Of all the frog species found in North America, wood frogs are probably the most able to withstand extreme cold weather. Other species that tolerate the cold include the gray treefrog, and spring peeper. All of these frogs may emerge from winter hibernation days or weeks earlier than other species, sometimes venturing out when there is still snow on the ground.

In conditions of extreme heat, frogs may also respond by retreating and seeking shelter. When it is too hot for their health, some frogs may also enter a state similar to hibernation, slowing down metabolism to conserve water. This state is referred to as "estivation."

HOME RANGE

"As I was riding out I heard a roaring before me, and I thought it was a bull in the bushes, on the other side of the dyke, though the sound was rather more hoarse than that of a bull."

— Peter Kalm (*Travels in North America,* 1749)

Most species of frogs in North America remain close to the spot where they hatched. Not only do they remain close to this "home" area throughout their adult lives, but they become very familiar with its physical features.

Adult frogs of many species learn the layout of the land as they feed and rest. Their memory of certain features — branches, rocks, holes, etc. — is a valuable aid in finding food, avoiding predators, and moving quickly in the dark without causing themselves injury. Other than a memorized map of their territory, odors may also provide important clues to frogs about objects around them.

The size of the territory used as a home base varies from species to species and may be influenced by the availability of food, climate, predators, and other variables. In general, the larger the frog, the more space it uses. For the largest species, such as bullfrogs, this area may be as much as 100 feet of shoreline; the smallest species, such as treefrogs, may occupy only a few feet as a home base. Studies of the range of a few species have produced some precise figures. Striped chorus frogs, for example, have ranges from less than 80 square feet to more than 700 square feet, with an average of about 250 square feet. The average range for the wood frog, at least in Michigan, is less than nine square feet. The average for green frogs (also in Michigan), is a little more than seven square feet.

Local conditions or the urge to breed can add more distance to the normal range of some frogs. Some move away from their home area during breeding, then return for the rest of the year. Individual frogs have been found more than one mile away from areas previously marked as their home base. When some young frogs are just emerging from the tadpole stage, they may also move away from their original home, as far as hundreds of feet or more than a mile if competition and crowding are a factor.

Many species of frogs maintain personal territories. They rely almost completely on sound to designate what is theirs and avoid what is not. Advertisement calls are the key, recognized by neighboring frogs and an effective marker of who is where. Frogs may venture out of their territory for breeding or feeding, yet when they are back in their home base, maintain its identity for outside frogs.

During cold seasons, when frogs are inactive or hibernating, they can have a different resting site than their warm weather home base. They travel between these two areas in relatively straight lines, according to some observers, and in most species that have been studied, return to their own individual territories year after year. How they make this kind of accurate migration is unknown, but the mechanism involved could be orientation to the light from the Sun. And some evidence has been found that in at least a few species, the southern cricket frog and the bullfrog are examples, frogs at night may be able to orient themselves from the moving positions of the stars and the Moon. The Sun or other celestial objects, however, are not part of the visual memory of frogs, but are keyed to another, non-visual sense, the pineal gland, which is sensitive to light but not connected to the eyes. However, biologists doubt that this kind of homing sense is used exclusively, as the frogs' movements are often carried out during rainy or overcast weather conditions, obscuring the skies. Smell may be more important, allowing frogs to recognize and home in on the unique odors attached to a familiar home base.

Frogs are generally nondiscriminating eaters, and large frogs will eat small frogs when given the chance. Nevertheless, different frog species are commonly found living closely together in the same habitats. Because they have different breeding habits and their tadpoles exploit different food resources in the local water sources, multiple species thrive together, despite the occasional danger from

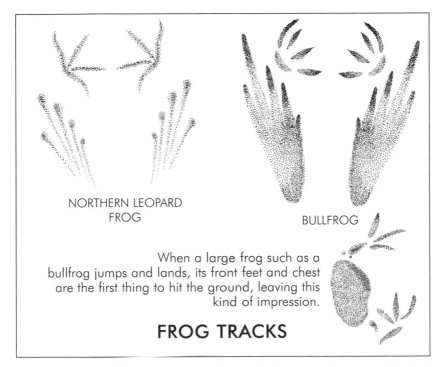

NORTHERN LEOPARD
FROG

BULLFROG

When a large frog such as a
bullfrog jumps and lands, its front feet and chest
are the first thing to hit the ground, leaving this
kind of impression.

FROG TRACKS

their larger neighbors. The number and density of species is linked to the amount of food in an area and the suitability for reproduction, both the direct result of the amount of rainfall. Studies have shown that frog populations have greater diversity of species the further south on the North American continent, which coincides with an increase in the amount of rainfall.

The highest density of species in North America is in Florida, Georgia, and other states in the extreme southeast. In certain locations, as many as fifty different kinds of amphibians are found, with about half of these being frogs and toads. At most North American locations, however, there are more likely to be only five to ten frog species in a given aquatic habitat. And because some of these species are more successful and aggressive than others, one or two species may make up the majority of the local frog population, the rest being minority residents.

FROG CALLS

"The tuneful frog nightly sings his evening song. There are no warblers that have more satisfaction in their songs."

— *Ellsworth Reporter* (Ellsworth, Kansas, May 21, 1874)

More often heard than seen, frogs have a known identity to humans because of the variation and uniqueness of their calls. From the deep booms of the bullfrog to the high-pitched drones of treefrogs, these calls are an important part of the existence of these animals.

Only the males are vocal in most frog species. The males of each species have a distinctive call, but even among the same species, frogs from one local geographic area may develop a slightly different call from the same frogs only a short distance away — a difference recognized by the frogs but not noticeable to the human observer. These group differences are much like geographic variations in the same human language, with accent, rhythm, and tones exhibiting minor changes. Biologists have found that frogs of the same species are able to identify these regional dialects.

Even within local ranges, some frogs seem to be able to identify each other by voice alone. Bullfrogs are one such example. They can recognize the calls of the neighboring frogs on the edges of their territory and will respond only to intruders whose voices are not known to them.

Calling not only makes a frog's presence known to any available females, it establishes the frog's territory to other male frogs. For this reason, biologists now refer to the frog's main vocalization as an "advertisement call." Previously, this could have been labeled either a mating call or a territorial call, but with the new description, it more accurately reflects the true function, to announce the frog's presence. Some frogs may have more than one pattern of advertisement call, altering the pattern according to the circumstances.

At some times of the year, frogs of some species may use one kind

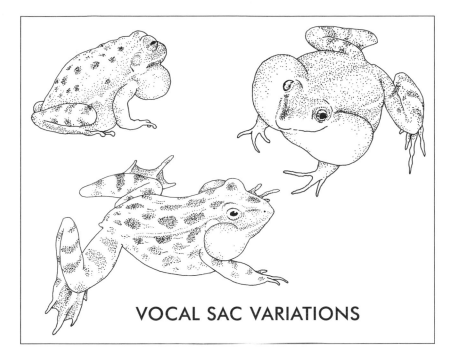

VOCAL SAC VARIATIONS

of advertisement call while they are stationed away from their breeding territory. They may have one kind of calling style that is solitary, used in these situations. Then, during the intense competition of the breeding season, they congregate in large numbers in temporary crowded conditions near the best sites for laying eggs. Competing with dozens or hundreds of other males within hearing range, they can also perform another advertisement call style, a chorus call, one designed to work in conjunction with a lot of other voices. For some species, chorus calls may also be used during nonbreeding seasons.

When frogs are temporarily crowded together in breeding groups, choruses can sound overwhelmingly dense, a combined din created by the overlapping calls of numerous individuals. But to the males that are part of the chorus and the females listening, individual voices must always carry through. The primary feature of frog choruses is a shared rhythm, an overall pattern of sound that turns the many calls into a symphony of sound, with individuals never lost within the group.

Choruses may involve frogs that maintain their territories and compete for females with minutely different sound patterns that allow females to identify a single male out of the blanket of sound. Frogs have a variety of methods for creating this kind of organized sound, mostly relying on rhythm and syncopation — one frog's calling pattern offset from others. In some choruses, one frog produces a dominant call and typically triggers a session of chorus calling just as a lead musical instrument may initiate a symphony. Choruses can be as small as two or three frogs and as large as thousands. But often, the calling sequence and nature of a single call within the chorus represents the dominance of that frog within the local population. Calling is linked to physical size and vigor, so that the lead frog in a chorus is often the strongest and most virile in the group.

Mating calls may be the primary means for dominant males to attract females and improve their reproductive success, rather than by combat or physical intimidation of other males, as is typical in other kinds of animals. But not all frog species rely on this kind of dominance. The females of some species select males based on characteristics that are linked to the control of the best breeding sites, such as the gray treefrog. And even when physical dominance is an important factor, lots of mating takes place among frogs other than the vocal masters.

Some male frogs are successful at mating without calling at all. These are called "satellite males." Lurking within a population of their own kind, they identify other males of their own species by the mating calls, selecting males with good territory and calling ability. They sneak into the territory of a calling male while the host is making his calls, but utter no calls of their own. When a female arrives, by chance she may encounter the satellite male instead of the host, permitting the interloper a silent advantage.

The vocal sounds produced by frogs originate from an air sac that is located on the bottom of the mouth. The air sac is inflated by pumping air into it from the lungs, and from there, back through

FROG CALL VARIETIES

BULLFROG	deep, resonant call
CASCADES FROG	rapid series of low, raspy notes
CRAWFISH FROG	deep, resonating trill
GOPHER FROG	deep-pitched snore
GREEN FROG	one or more twangy notes
FLORIDA LEOPARD FROG	series of short, gruff croaks
NORTHERN LEOPARD FROG	deep rattling snore
PLAINS LEOPARD FROG	series of guttural chucks
MINK FROG	series of deep, rough notes
OREGON SPOTTED FROG	series of short croaks
PICKEREL FROG	deep snoring notes
PIG FROG	short, pig-like grunts
RED-LEGGED FROG	series of thin, rough notes
RIVER FROG	deep prolonged snoring notes
WOOD FROG	series of short, quack-like notes
NORTHERN CRICKET FROG	high, rhythmic clicking
BARKING TREEFROG	series of barking notes
BIRD-VOICED TREEFROG	short, bird-like whistles
GRAY TREEFROG	high, slow musical trill
GREEN TREEFROG	ringing bell-like notes
PACIFIC TREEFROG	high double notes
SQUIRREL TREEFROG	raspy, squirrel-like notes
BOREAL CHORUS FROG	notes like plucked teeth of comb
BRIMLEY'S CHORUS FROG	short, raspy trilled notes
LITTLE GRASS FROG	high thin tinkling notes
MOUNTAIN CHORUS FROG	high squeaky notes
SOUTHERN CHORUS FROG	raspy musical trill
SPRING PEEPER	high-pitched peeps
UPLAND CHORUS FROG	raspy trill
WESTERN CHORUS FROG	raspy trill rising in pitch

the mouth. Some frogs produce a continuous call by shuttling the same pocket of air from the lungs to the air sac and back to the lungs.

The air sac not only produces the force behind a call, it helps amplify the sound by acting as a resonator. Much like the bodies of stringed instruments, the hollow structure produces sympathetic vibrations that add up to a louder volume than if the sound were produced without the sac.

Frogs use a lot of energy to generate their calls. Particularly for the smallest species, males must consume a lot of food in order to keep up their vocalizations, especially during the breeding season. Research on wood frogs shows that the males get this energy entirely from glycogen stored in their bodies. Glycogen is a form of glucose, a natural sugar, and can be readily converted to energy. Wood frogs are a species that has a short, concentrated breeding season, lasting only a few days, and this kind of energy source is efficient for their use. On the other hand, spring peepers may be involved in breeding for a period up to a few months long, requiring a different kind of energy source for their calls. With these frogs, an estimated 90 percent of the energy requirements for vocalizations come from stored lipids, compounds that release energy more slowly than glycogen.

Because mating calls are so critical to the survival of most frog species, the physical structure that involves making vocalizations can take up a large part of a frog's anatomy. The muscles used in vocalizing by spring peeper males, for example, may be 15 percent of the total body mass of the frog. The same muscles in female spring peepers, on the other hand, take up only 3 percent of body mass.

The energy used to make mating calls may also put a tremendous demand on a frog's body. A study of gray treefrogs during the mating season indicated their rate of oxygen consumption was seven times more than when they were at rest.

Frogs calls can be measured in a variety of frequencies. Mature bullfrogs call at about 300 Hz, the lowest end of the spectrum for

North American species. Spring peepers, on the other hand, are at the high end of the spectrum, calling at about 3,000 Hz. The calls can also vary considerably in length, with the longest lasting for up to ten seconds and the shortest, such as that from the cricket frog, lasting only a tenth of a second.

On the receiving end, female frogs are clearly capable of identifying potential mates. The efficiency with which frogs reproduce is one measure of this success. Biologists, however, are somewhat puzzled by a major inefficiency of frog anatomy, a deficiency in the design of their ears, apparently handicapping their ability to precisely locate where sounds are coming from. If they can't pinpoint the source of a mating call, after all, it would be difficult for the females to find the male that is making it. The problem lies mostly in the placement of the frog's ears, too close together to permit accurate comparison of sound waves, a process similar to that in eyes, which rely on binocular vision to fix locations and distances. Frog ears are also unable to hear very high frequencies where sound

FOLK CALLS

The bullfrog has one of the most distinctive calls of all frogs in North America. For generations, people have identified this sound with a variety of English words and phrases such as "jug-o-rum," and "be drowned." One folk method of telling the age of a bullfrog by the sound of its calls suggests this analogy ...

The baby bullfrog says "ankle deep, ankle deep."

Little brother bullfrog says "knee deep, knee deep."

Big brother bullfrog says "thigh high, thigh high."

The daddy bullfrog says "too deep, too deep."

And the granddaddy bullfrog says "better go round, better go round."

FOREIGN FROG CALLS

In English, the generic sound of a frog call is often written as "croak" or "ribbit," but in other languages and cultures, there is a wide variety of other words for this sound.

AFRIKAANS kwaak-kwaak

ARABIC gar gar

CHINESE MANDARIN guo guo

CROATIAN kre-kre

DUTCH kwak kwak

ESTONIAN krooks-krooks

FINNISH kvak kvak

FRENCH coa-coa

GERMAN quaak quaak

HEBREW kwa kwa

HINDI me:ko:me:k-me:ko:me:k

HUNGARIAN bre-ke-ke

ITALIAN cra cra

JAPANESE kerokero

KOREAN gae-gool-gae-gool

RUSSIAN kva-kva

SPANISH (SPAIN) cruá-cruá

SPANISH (PERU) croac, croac

SWEDISH kvack

THAI ob ob (with high tone)

TURKISH vrak vrak

UKRAINIAN kwa-kwa

This list was created by Catherine N. Ball and published with permission. ©1996–1998 Catherine N. Ball.

waves are short. These frequencies work best when used for sound location. Bats, for example, use ultra-high frequency sound waves to locate insects in the air, even in darkness.

Frogs make up for this deficiency in anatomy with other systems for processing sound. One of these is an open connection between the ear canals by way of the mouth, allowing the same sound waves to hit the eardrum twice, the second time out of sync with the first. Some biologists believe that instead of the standard kind of stereo sound comparison, frogs are able to figure distance and location by judging how the same sounds hit each ear. Another recent discovery is a "vibration spot" located near the lungs in some frog species. This spot has been found to vibrate in tune with the frog's eardrums, possibly producing an additional source of measurement for a sound source.

The vocalizations produced by different species can vary in several ways. Some calls are optimized for carrying over long distances, while others have sound wave features that carry well only for a few yards. Green frog calls, for example, carry up to half a mile.

As a rule of thumb, frogs that produce the loudest sounds as a group are those that breed around temporary bodies of water. Driven by the need to mate, lay eggs, and allow their tadpoles to develop before the water disappears, these kinds of frogs — found in arid climates as well as locations affected by intense rainy seasons — have developed a more frantic mating style than others, with a sound level to match.

In wet climates, rain forests, and wetlands where temperatures are above freezing year round, competing frog species often have overlapping ranges. This condition has led to the development of calls that can be heard through the background noise created by all of the other frogs in the environment. Frog species that compete in these kinds of amphibian-rich environments may have calls that focus on different frequencies, vary over a range of frequencies, and are produced at different volumes.

A few frog species have also developed another way to overcome competing noises. They make their calls while fully submerged, sending vocal signals entirely through the water. The red-legged frog, the foothill yellow-legged frog, and the Ramsey Canyon leopard frog are species that make advertising calls while submerged.

Female bullfrogs are one of the few exceptions to the rule that only male frogs vocalize. These females have a call similar to male bullfrogs, used mostly for aggression when encountering other frogs entering their territory. They have also been observed calling in choruses during the reproductive season. Female carpenter frogs also may make calls when they are breeding.

Many frogs also have another kind of call that signals panic or alarm and is triggered by predators, often when the frogs have been physically grabbed. Humans who handle frogs may also create this

FROG CALL GUIDES

Recordings of the calls of various frog species can be found on many sites on the World Wide Web, especially those hosted by state wildlife agencies (see *Online Resources*, page 174). Commercial recordings are also available.

Sounds of North American Frogs. A compact disc with the calls of 57 species of North American frogs and toads is available from Smithsonian Folkways (release #45060).
202-287-7298
http://www.si.edu/folkways/frogsbut.htm/

The Calls of Frogs and Toads. A taped cassette or compact disc with the calls of 42 species of frogs and toads native to the eastern states, available from Northword Nature Guides.
800-336-5666

Voices of the Night. A tape cassette with the calls of 36 species of frogs and toads of eastern North America is available from the Library of Natural Sound at the Cornell Laboratory of Ornithology. http://birds.cornell.edu/LNS/LNS.htm/

Frog and Toad Calls of the Pacific Coast. Also from the Library of Natural Sound, this title is available as a tape cassette or compact disc and includes calls from 25 species found in the Pacific northwest.

reaction. This kind of panic or distress call may help in species iden-tification, as different kinds of frogs often make distinctive sounds in this situation. Females as well as males may make these calls, even some juveniles. In addition, female frogs in many species make what is referred to as a "release call," a special sound intended to signal males that are grasping them in mating, a vocal order to cease amplexus, the name for this position.

FROG DISEASES

"Can I unmoved see thee dying
On a log,
Expiring frog!" — Charles Dickens (*Pickwick Papers,* 1837)

Even before they become adult frogs, tadpoles can be subject to diseases or toxic damage from their environment. Eggs, too, are vulnerable. A few species of insects seek out frog eggs when they are freshly laid and use them as hatching sites for their own eggs. As the insect larvae develop, they become parasites, eating the frog eggs. Some frogs, in response, have developed behavior to guard their eggs against intrusions by insects, making a meal of any that get too close. Those frog eggs that are parasitized typically develop unnatural shapes, making them stick out from the mass of eggs around them. Mother frogs of some species can spot these deformed eggs and may eat them, keeping the parasites from creating further damage if the eggs had hatched.

Individual frogs can become afflicted with a wide variety of ailments. Viral infections, tuberculosis, cancer, and attacks by a host of bacteria and fungi are part of the threat from their natural environment. One of the most common ailments that affects frogs is red-leg disease. As the name suggests, this affliction results in legs that are swollen and reddish in color. Several types of bacteria have been linked to this disease, which may result in death.

Frogs can also contract salmonella bacteria from the soil or food that they eat, and it is thought to be common in many populations. Ordinarily, however, it is harbored in relatively small quantities by a frog's digestive system without causing any problems. During times of stress, this balance can be upset, resulting in serious illness and death.

Other organisms hosted by frogs include E. coli, pseudomonas, mycobacterium marinum, and aeromonas, all infectious agents that may be carried without causing a frog any harm. If touched by humans, however, any of these might be picked up and create a serious infection for the careless handler.

Even though frogs live in damp conditions, fungal infections rarely affect them unless other injuries, such as skin abrasions or cuts, trigger rapid growth. This may be because of unique properties in their skin or the protective result of compounds naturally produced by their skin glands.

Frogs are hosts to tapeworms, nematodes, roundworms, flukes, leeches, ticks, mites, fish lice, and other parasites, which in most habitats remain in balance, killing a few frogs but not endangering an entire population.

In recent years, frogs have been a popular media subject as reports increase about malformed frogs found in some areas of North America. Malformations, which include extra or missing limbs, are a natural part of the life cycle of frogs, occurring as a result of disease, natural toxins, and genetic mutations. The new reports, however, indicate that there are new threats to frogs from human-induced changes in their habitats, primarily pollution. For more information about frog malformations, see "Endangered Frogs" on page 168.

LONGEVITY

Due to a precarious existence in the wild, most frogs don't live very long, a few years on average. But if they escape being eaten, some frogs can live for more than ten years. In captivity, a bullfrog has lived for more than fifteen years and cricket frogs for more than five years.

PEOPLE VS. FROGS

"In fact the enemies of the little frog are legion, one of the worst being Man. In France, Italy, and other parts of the Continent, the skinned fleshy hind-limbs are turned into a by no means disagreeable ragoût, or into dainty morsels when fried in butter and encrusted with bread-crumbs."

— Hans Gadow (*The Cambridge Natural History, Vol. III, Amphibia and Reptiles*, 1901)

Even when not eaten, frogs have long been demeaned as a large and essentially valueless part of the natural environment. As such, frogs, along with birds and almost all small mammals and reptiles, have been a traditional target for recreational shooting. In the early days of the development of the Americas by Europeans, when frogs were not being hunted for food, they were often being "plinked" at for target practice. This excerpt from a newspaper in the Kansas territory in 1876 describes such activity.

"I hear of a good many frogs being shot nowadays, well, they are good eating if cooked right, but I guess the sportsmen are only practicing [sic] on the frogs until such time as it is lawful to shoot chickens ..."

Although some people have biases against the meat of frogs, there is a long tradition of exploiting these amphibians as food. In many parts of the world, including North America and Europe, frogs are sought after as a staple, even a delicacy. In some cultures, frogs have long been raised in captivity to provide a steady supply of meat. The majority of the contemporary population may never encounter a frog unless it is with the thought of consumption in mind.

In many different cultures around the world, frogs, particularly their legs, have a significant place in the human diet. Frogs are roasted over open fires, fried in pans, smoked, braised, sauteed, chopped, stewed, steamed, and added to soups. In some cultures, tadpoles are gathered and eaten as well, with a similar variety of cooking methods.

Sometimes frogs are collected as an animal of opportunity, when other food is not available; mostly, hunting was an activity focused to take advantage of the frogs' peak breeding season. But long before the modern French menu created a classy image of frogs' legs as a gourmet food, people have also found ways to control its reproduction for their own benefit. In the Amazon River system of South America, for example, the Tukano Indians have a traditional method they use to provide a dependable supply of frogs. There, a local species of frog known as "omá" is bred in pools that are dug into the banks of streams. During the rainy season, flooding river water rises and fills the pools; following the end of the rains, the water trapped in the pools becomes a breeding site for the frogs.

The Guiana Indians in South America also breed frogs for food, digging pits in the bottom of small ponds. They line the pits with grass that creates a platform on which captive frogs lay their eggs. The Guianas eat these frogs as well as their tadpoles and eggs. One occupational hazard, however, threatens anyone who seeks out frog eggs for food, particularly in Central and South America. People may get deathly ill and die from their finds because of mistaken identity; the eggs they discover may come from species which have toxic compounds in their eggs.

Accidental poisoning from frog eggs, tadpoles, or frogs is also an occasional occurrence in North America. Seasoned frog eaters generally eat only the legs and remove the skin first, eliminating the primary source of danger.

The Aztecs, Incas, and Mayans all included frogs and tadpoles as part of their diets, but as seasonal food only. Some of their ceremonial dishes were made with frogs and if certain festivals coincided with the right season for frogs, they were part of the menu. One recipe featured tadpoles prepared by frying them with ground corn and dried spirulina, an edible algae gathered in fresh water.

In New Guinea, frogs are a major source of food for many of the

FROG SPEAR.

No. 81750. Frog spear, 3 tines, with socket to put pole in. Each.........15c.

Entry published in the 1897 *Sears Roebuck Catalogue*.

native cultures. The Karam people, located in the western Highlands, have well-developed skills and techniques for catching local frog species. They cut and burn brush to create open areas into which frogs venture. Hunters also identify and locate individual frogs by their calls and even train their dogs to join in the hunt.

In modern times in North America, most commercial use of frogs for meat relies on the legs of three species, the bullfrog, the green frog, and the northern leopard frog. Favorite recipes include deep frying, sauteeing, and baking, with regional variations. In parts of the southeast and south, where frogs are most often used as food, local sauces — especially those based on hot peppers — have also become part of the tradition of eating this meat.

Where frogs are on the menu, frog hunting prospers, although commercial frog farms have eclipsed hunting as the major source in recent decades. Frog gigging is the traditional hunting method of choice, with a lantern or spotlight used to transfix the frog while the hunter spears it with a lance tipped with a two- or three-pronged gig designed for this prey. Some hunters prefer catching their prey by hand, but still rely on the light to keep the targeted frog frozen in place. Another traditional method of snagging frogs relies on a fishing pole rigged with a line and a small square of fabric or fur. Twitching this lure in front of the target, the frog snatches the lure and usually holds on in the mistaken belief that it has grabbed its own dinner instead of the other way around.

Even though frogs have long been popular as a food source for people, it is not the only reason they have been hunted. For several hundred years, frogs have been a major source of scientific study, used for medical research in a broad array of specialities. Anton van Leeuwenhoek (1632–1723), who is credited with the invention of the microscope, used it early on to delve into the mysteries of the animal body, using tadpoles and frogs as his subjects. In 1688, he was the first to discover the capillaries in the gills of the tadpole, and an Italian anatomist, Marcello Malpighi (1628–1694) also found new discoveries about the structure of lungs by using an early microscope to peer at those of frogs. The focus of these microscopists' attention helped revolutionize medicine. Frogs were instrumental in the discovery and exploration of blood vessels in animals, many invisible to the naked eye, and the action of the blood as it flows through them. And from the earliest days of the microscope, frogs have been studied alive as well as dead.

> "If care be taken to exclude every frog and salamander from a spring, it will be found that very soon the water will not be so pure, however strong the current, as is that of a frog-frequented spring."
> — Charles C. Abbott
> (A Naturalist's Rambles About Home, 1884)

In the late 1700s, Luigi Galvani (1737–1798), an Italian doctor, created and performed his now famous experiments, applying jolts of electricity to the severed legs of frogs. Not only did he discover that electricity might be involved in the transmission of nerve impulses, it was one of the first demonstrations of the power and potential of electricity, a discovery that prompted further experiments by Alessandro Volta, one of the founders of electrical theory.

By this time, frogs were in wide use as anatomical models for biologists, anatomists, and doctors. In 1864, the first book on frog anatomy, *Anatomie des Frosches*, by Alexander Ecker, was published. By the beginning of the twentieth century, frog dissection and reproduction had become an essential part of the teaching curriculum of most secondary schools, colleges, and medical schools in North America. In scientific laboratories, frog research focused on many subjects, including eyesight, nerve growth, and blood flow. Major medical breakthroughs that have developed from frog research include the first demonstration of a neurotransmitter, the role of fevers in preventing the spread of infections, and the toxicity of natural and synthetic compounds. Present research programs are focusing on the skin secretions of a variety of frogs and toads, including those that are extremely poisonous. Initial results suggest that compounds derived from some of these secretions may be useful in medical treatments, including combating certain types of brain diseases and the suppression of pain.

In recent decades, the use of frogs for education and research have involved as many as 10 million frogs a year. Although most of these frogs come from commercial frog farms, their use has been increasingly criticized as an unnecessary threat to their future, if not an inappropriate use of animal lifeforms. One of the biggest arguments here comes from the handling methods used by this industry. Typically, during holding and shipping of large numbers of live frogs,

VIRTUAL FROGS

Frog anatomy can now be explored with a computer. Interactive digital models of frogs are available on CD-ROMs from a number of sources.

Digital Frog CD-ROM
Tangent Scientific 800-363-2908
http://www.tangentscientific.com/default.eht/

Digital Frog CD-ROM
Digital Frog International Inc. 800-621-3764
http://www.digitalfrog.com/

Dissectionworks interactive frog CD-ROM
Carolina Biological Supply Company 800-334-5551
http://www.carosci.com/

Technical Dissection Simulations CD-ROM
Science Class 800-478-8476
http://www.scienceclass.com/

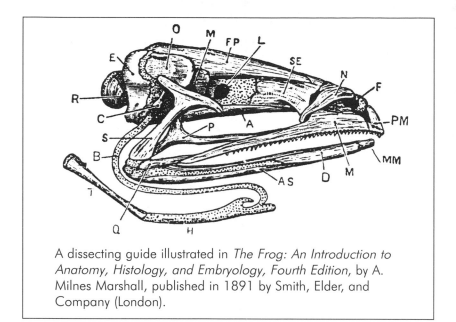

A dissecting guide illustrated in *The Frog: An Introduction to Anatomy, Histology, and Embryology, Fourth Edition*, by A. Milnes Marshall, published in 1891 by Smith, Elder, and Company (London).

they are crammed together in sacks, resulting in stress, injuries, and the premature death of a large percentage of the animals shipped.

In recent decades, public concern has also increased regarding the use of live animals for medical experiments, health tests, and dissection in schools. Although frogs have not received as much attention as mammals, such as monkeys, cats, and dogs, they are becoming less "politically correct" as this movement progresses. The development of alternatives has provided some options. Artificial frog models provide realistic depictions of their anatomy, and the creation of interactive digital models of the frog provides a computerized dissecting experience that is close to the real thing, at least minimally being able to fulfill the mission of teaching introductory biology.

Another relatively modern trend is the use of frogs and toads as exotic pets. Although no one knows for sure, there may be hundreds of thousands of native, common, and rare species kept in homes and offices throughout the world. Some native species are not threatened in the wild and thrive in artificial environments, living ten or more years. In a few cases, toads have lived more than thirty years in captivity. Exploitation of rare frogs from around the world, however, has been part of this consumer movement. In recent years, along with other rare and exotic amphibians, reptiles, birds, and mammals, national and international regulations have been gradually strengthened to help control improper importation. Responsible pet owners have also created a new philosophy that identifies the value and necessity of keeping rare animals free in their wild environments. To fulfill the demand for exotic species, frogs are supplied only from captive breeding.

Past lapses in judgment by some exotic frog owners have also created local environmental problems in a few places. Captive frogs that were imported from other areas of the world have escaped or been deliberately dumped, and where the local environment supports them, began establishing self-sustaining populations. The African clawed frog is an example of this kind and is now a permanent resident in parts of southern California, displacing native frogs as its population spreads. Although these frogs may survive, their success is not shared by other animals in their new home range, particularly the frogs that were already there, adapted by thousands or tens of thousands of years to the ecological niche in which they live.

Another effect that frogs may have on humans comes from the sky. Although rare, many places around the world have been the site of a literal rain of frogs. These unusual occurrences have been noted in 1804 near Toulouse, France; in 1873 near Kansas City, Missouri (reported in the *Scientific American*); and in 1892 near Birmingham, England, among others. Although no one has officially explained how such mass droppings happened, it is likely that windstorms, tornadoes, or other weather phenomenon could have been responsible. Individual frogs have dropped from the sky as well, although these could well be the result of a bird dropping its prey while in flight.

ENDANGERED FROGS

"What claims, it may be asked, have these frogs upon us? This is easily answered. They are not only great checks upon an undue increase of insect life, but they are also scavengers."
— Charles C. Abbott
(A Naturalist's Rambles About Home, 1884)

Frogs are not faring well in the modern era. The spread of civilization is reducing and destroying their natural habitats, and the pollution generated by urban growth is poisoning that which is left. Even where frogs are relatively unaffected by civilization, mankind has introduced new threats, accidentally and deliberately transporting non-native frog species into new areas, where they upset the balance of nature.

In North America, one of the greatest frog threats comes from this kind of mismanagement. Bullfrogs, the largest and one of the most aggressive frog species, have been introduced into areas far beyond the fringes of their original range, which was mostly territory east of the Mississippi River. In western states, outside of the original range, the introduction of bullfrogs has been carried out for decades. The bullfrogs have benefited, thriving in most of the habitats where they are placed. But as this species has gained, it has been at the expense of frogs that were already naturally established. Unable to compete with the larger and more aggressive bullfrogs for territory or food, populations of some native species have become threatened. In many cases, the bullfrogs also eat the smaller resident frogs.

Loss of habitat is the single biggest known threat to frogs and other amphibians, and a decrease in wetlands is the major cause of this shrinkage. Farming and urban uses have removed most of this traditional breeding ground, from 50 to more than 90 percent in some parts of the United States and Canada. And even when ponds, marshes, and other wetlands are left undeveloped, they are increasingly isolated from one another, becoming remote ecological islands surrounded by barriers that amphibians are often not able to cross, limiting the ability of natural populations to migrate or add new members to local populations. With fewer places to live, fewer frogs are living.

With the increasing presence of people, roads and traffic arteries present a major threat to frogs. One study in Ontario, for example, counted more than 10,000 leopard frogs killed in a single year along a section of road that was only two-and-a-half miles long. How people use nonurban areas also has a negative effect on frogs. Off-road vehicles and camping, for example, can produce stress, disrupt breeding activities, and alter frog habitats.

In many of the remaining natural areas, however, frog populations are thriving. But for more than a decade, scientists around the world have reported that many species of amphibians have suffered declines in population even within the supposed safety of their home ranges. In a few cases, some species have already become extinct. Although large-scale efforts have been mounted to measure and study this problem, there are as yet few common themes emerging as culprits in this ecological mystery.

Part of the problem in identifying what is happening to the world's amphibians is a lack of knowledge of what normally happens in healthy amphibian populations. For many species, including some that are currently in decline, benchmark statistics are not available for comparison. This can be a problem, because in many kinds of animals, extreme variations in population size are normal and do not indicate problems. With the population decline for frogs, however, biologists are certain that something more than natural population variation is underway, at least in some cases.

One recent study, for example, focused on environmental threats to northern leopard frogs, a species known to be declining in parts of its natural range. In aquatic habitats where these frogs live, acidity levels higher than pH 5.5 were found to kill more than 60 percent of all frogs within ten days of exposure. This level of acidity can come from pollution in ground water, surface water, or acid rain.

Despite the problems in assessment, enough is known about some species of frogs to raise concern. In North America, frog species that are currently experiencing serious population declines include:

Cascades frog (*Rana cascadae*)

Chiricahua leopard frog (*Rana chiricahuensis*)

Columbia spotted frog (*Rana luteiventris*)

foothill yellow-legged frog (*Rana boylii*)

lowland leopard frog (*Rana yavapaiensis*)

mountain yellow-legged frog (*Rana muscosa*)

northern leopard frog (*Rana pipiens*)

Oregon spotted frog (*Rana pretiosa*)

plains leopard frog (*Rana blairi*)

Ramsey Canyon leopard frog (*Rana subaquavocalis*)

red-legged frog (*Rana aurora*)

Tarahumara frog (*Rana tarahumarae*)

Toads and newts are also declining, often in different areas than those where frogs have been affected.

At the same time that unnatural population declines are apparently happening, the number of deformed frogs and other amphibians is increasing, sometimes in the same geographic areas as the declines, but not always. Deformities to tadpoles and frogs are not unknown in unspoiled, natural environments, but the current trend is most likely linked to excessive amounts of toxic materials found somewhere in the habitat or feeding chain of the animals affected. Malformations that are typical include missing or displaced eyes, tadpole tails retained in adults, split or disfigured limbs, missing limbs, extra limbs, partial limbs, missing digits, extra digits, malformed webbing, and various disfigurements of the head, jaw, or body.

Widespread monitoring programs are underway — with active involvement from students, volunteers, and amateur observers — to gather more evidence of this unnatural phenomenon and create a database of locations and spread. But even while attracting new

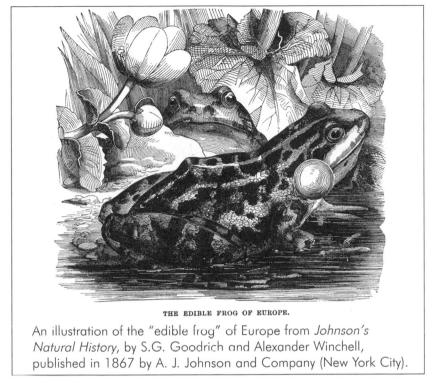

THE EDIBLE FROG OF EUROPE.

An illustration of the "edible frog" of Europe from *Johnson's Natural History*, by S.G. Goodrich and Alexander Winchell, published in 1867 by A. J. Johnson and Company (New York City).

attention, historical records indicate it may not be all that unusual. Scientific records of malformed frogs date back to 1740 and cover twenty-four states, two provinces in Canada, and many foreign countries. In the most recent period of observations of these abnormalities, most have been concentrated in a geographical region that runs through the upper midwestern states. Other parts of the country either have many fewer reports or none at all.

Compounds produced by human activity are a major part of the threat facing frogs. These include pesticides, insecticides, fertilizers, fungicides, industrial pollution, automotive emissions, and heavy metals. The transmission of these harmful agents to frog habitats can come from agricultural runoff, leakage from garbage dumps or industrial sites, ground water contamination, storm sewers, and acid rain.

171

A decline in the number of frogs and the number of frog species is not just a problem for frog lovers. Frogs and other amphibians, because of their physiology and intimate interaction with the environment, function as a unique type of "bio-indicator" that represents an early warning system, a signal of decreasing environmental health that appears before the degradation begins to affect other animals, including humans. Unfortunately for frogs and other amphibians, they are very good bio-indicators.

FROGS AS BIO-INDICATORS

Characteristics of frogs that make them a target for environmental ills before other animals include:

- **The nature of their skin**. It absorbs water, other liquids, and gases.

- **The nature of their eggs and larvae**. They are sensitive to the amount of ultraviolet light transmitted through the atmosphere and sensitive to unnatural chemicals during metamorphosis that may mimic and alter natural growth cycles.

- **Their eating habits**. Tadpoles consume large amounts of organic material and adults eat large numbers of insects and other small animals, concentrating toxins contained in this food.

- **Their habitats**. Many species have specialized habits and physiology that are adapted for certain habitats, especially wetlands. When this habitat is reduced, removed, altered, or polluted, entire populations may disappear.

RESOURCES

ORGANIZATIONS AND PROGRAMS

American Society of Ichthyologists and Herpetologists. University of Texas, J.J. Pickle Research Campus. Texas Natural History Collections, Building 176, 10100 Burnet Road, Austin, TX 78758-4445 512-471-0995 http://www.utexas.edu/depts/asih/

Amphibian Conservation Alliance. 563 Martin Street, Oakland, CA 94609 510-653-6006 EMAIL aca@frogs.org http://www.frogs.org/home.htm

Canadian Amphibian and Reptile Conservation Network 250-595-7556 http://www.cciw.ca/ecowatch/dapcan/carc_net.htm/

Center for North American Amphibians and Reptiles 1502 Medinah Circle, Lawrence, KS 66047 785-749-3467 http://eagle.cc.ukans.edu/~cnaar/CNAARHomePage.html/

International Society for the Study and Conservation of Amphibians Department of Biological and Environmental Sciences Lake Charles, LA 70605-2000

North American Amphibian Monitoring Program http://www.im.nbs.gov/amphibs.html/

North American Reporting Center for Amphibian Malformations Northern Prairie Wildlife Research Center, Biological Resources Division U.S. Geological Survey 800-238-9801

PERIODICALS

Froglog. Newsletter of the Declining Amphibian Populations Task force. http://acs-info.open.ac.uk/info/newsletters/FROGLOG.html/

Herpetologica. Publication of the Herpetologists' League, available with membership. The Herpetologists' League, c/o Department of Biological Sciences Box 70726, East Tennessee State University, Johnson City, TN 37614-0726 http://130.160.104.76/HL/

Herpetological Review. Newsletter published by the Society for the Study of Amphibians and Reptiles, available with membership. Society for the Study of Amphibians and Reptiles. c/o Department of Biology, St. Louis University, 3507 Laclede, St. Louis, MO 63103-2010

Journal of Herpetology. A quarterly publication of the Society for the Study of Amphibians and Reptiles, available with membership. Society for the Study of Amphibians and Reptiles, c/o Department of Biology, St. Louis University, 3507 Laclede, St. Louis, MO 63103-2010

ONLINE RESOURCES

To find useful and interesting information about frogs on the World Wide Web, use a search program and keywords such as "frog," "toad," or "amphibian." For a more targeted search, use additional keywords such as the common or scientific name of a species of frog or the name of a country, state, or wilderness area. Also, try Web pages hosted by state wildlife departments, museums, wildlife preserves, zoos, and other animal organizations..

American Society of Ichthyologists and Herpetologists
http://www.utexas.edu/depts/asih/

Amphibian Conservation Alliance. http://www.frogs.org/home.htm/

Canadian Amphibian and Reptile Conservation Network.
http://www.cciw.ca/ecowatch/dapcan/carc_net.htm/

Center for North American Amphibians and Reptiles.
http://eagle.cc.ukans.edu/~cnaar/CNAARHomePage.html/

The Herpetologists' League. http://130.160.104.76/HL/

The Herptox Page. http://www.cciw.ca/green-lane/herptox/

National Wildlife Federation. http://www.nwf.org/nwf/index.html/

The Nature Conservancy. http://www.tnc.org/

North American Amphibian Monitoring Program.
http://www.im.nbs.gov/amphib.html/

U.S. Fish and Wildlife Service. http://www.fws.gov/

FIELD GUIDES

Several major series of field guides include titles on the amphibians of North America. Readers should be aware that not all publishers have yet adopted the latest scientific naming and organization for frogs, as used in this book.

Field Guide to the Reptiles and Amphibians of Eastern and Central North America, by Roger Conant. 1998, Peterson Field Guide Series, Houghton Mifflin Company.

Field Guide to Western Reptiles and Amphibians, by Robert C. Stebbins. 1998, Peterson Field Guide Series, Houghton Mifflin Company.

Guide to Amphibians and Reptiles, by Thomas F. Tyning. 1990, Stokes Nature Guides.

Handbook of Frogs and Toads, by Albert Hazen Wright and Anna Allen Wright. 1949, 1965, Cornell University Press.

National Audubon Society Field Guide to North American Reptiles and Amphibians, by John L. Behler and F. Wayne King. 1997, Alfred A. Knopf.

BIBLIOGRAPHY

Beebee, T.J.C. *Ecology and Conservation of Amphibians*. 1996, Chapman & Hall (London, England).

Caras, Roger A. *Dangerous to Man, Wild Animals: A Definitive Study of Their Reputed Dangers to Man*. 1964, Chilton Books (Philadelphia, PA).

Collins, Joseph T., editor. *Standard Common and Current Scientific Names for North American Amphibians and Reptiles, Third Edition*. 1990, Society for the Study of Amphibians and Reptiles.

Cook, Francis R. *Introduction to Canadian Amphibians and Reptiles*. 1984, National Museum of Natural Science/National Museums of Canada.

Degenhardt, William G., Painter, Charles W., and Price, Andrew H. *Amphibians and Reptiles of New Mexico*. 1996, University of New Mexico Press (Albuquerque, NM).

DeLys, Claudia. *A Treasury of American Superstitions*. 1948, Philosophical Library (New York, NY). Republished as *A Treasury of Superstitions* in 1997 by Gramercy Books/Random House.

Duellman, William E. and Trueb, Linda. *Biology of Amphibians*. 1986, McGraw-Hill Book Company.

Fite, Katherine V., editor. *The Amphibian Visual System: A Multidisciplinary Approach*. 1976, Academic Press Inc.

Fleharty, Eugene D. *Wild Animals and Settlers on the Great Plains*. 1995, University of Oklahoma Press (Norman, OK).

Fort, Charles. *The Book of the Damned*. 1919, Boni and Liveright (London). Republished in 1941 by Holt, Rinehart and Winston.

Gilbert, Stephen G. *Pictorial Anatomy of the Frog*. 1965, University of Washington Press.

Gray, James. *Animal Locomotion*. 1968, W. W. Norton and Company.

Halliday, Tim R. and Adler, Kraig, editors. *The Encyclopedia of Reptiles and Amphibians*. 1986, Facts on File Inc.

Harding, James H. *Amphibians and Reptiles of the Great Lakes Region*. 1997, University of Michigan Press (Ann Arbor, MI).

Hart, Stephen. *The Language of Animals*. 1996, Henry Holt and Company.

Jaeger, Edmund C. *A Sourcebook of Biological Names and Terms, Third Edition*. 1955, Charles C. Thomas, Publisher (Springfield, IL).

Jones, Gertrude. *Dictionary of Mythology, Folklore, and Symbols*. 1961, Scarecrow Press, Inc.

Kavasch, E. Barrie. *Enduring Harvests: Native American Foods and Festivals for Every Season*. 1995, Globe Pequot Press.

Liner, Ernest A. *Scientific and Common Names for the Amphibians and Reptiles of Mexico in English and Spanish*. 1994, Society for the Study of Amphibians and Reptiles.

Mason, George F. *Animal Vision*. 1968, William Morrow and Company.

Oliver, James A. *The Natural History of North American Amphibians and Reptiles*. 1955, D. Van Nostrand Company Inc.

Parsons, Elsie Clews. *Pueblo Indian Religion*. 1939, University of Chicago Press. Republished in 1966 by Bison Books/University of Nebraska Press.

Pough, F. Harvey. *Herpetology*. 1998, Prentice-Hall.

Puckett, Newbell Niles. *Popular Beliefs and Superstitions: A Compendium of American Folklore*. 1981, G.K. Hall & Company (Boston, MA).

Sax, Boria. *The Frog King: On Legends, Fables, Fairy Tales and Anecdotes of Animals*. 1990, Pace University Press (New York, NY).

Schmidt-Nielsen, Knut. *Animal Physiology: Adaptation and Environment*. 1975, Cambridge University Press.

Society for the Study of Amphibians and Reptiles, editors. *Catalogue of American Amphibians and Reptiles*. 1971, Society for the Study of Amphibians and Reptiles.

Stebbins, Robert C. *Amphibians and Reptiles of California*. 1972, University of California Press (Berkeley, CA).

Stebbins, Robert C. and Cohen, Nathan W. *A Natural History of Amphibians*. 1995, Princeton University Press.

Tulin, Melissa S. *Aardvarks to Zebras: A Menageree of Facts, Fiction, and Fantasy About the Wonderful World of Animals*. 1995, MJF Books (New York).

Tyler, Michael J. *Frogs*. 1976, Collins Ltd. (Sydney, Australia).

Walker, Deward E. Jr. *Blood of the Monster: The Nez Perce Coyote Cycle*. 1994, High Plains Publishing Company (Worland, WY).

Wright, Albert Hazen and Wright, Anna Allen. *Handbook of Frogs and Toads*. 1949, 1965, Cornell University Press.

INDEX

179

181